FREEDOM OF INFORMATION
...FREEDOM OF THE INDIVIDUAL?

DAYS OF DECISION

Series Editor: Julia Neuberger

FREEDOM OF INFORMATION

...FREEDOM OF THE INDIVIDUAL?

PAPERMAC

First published 1987 by
PAPERMAC
a division of Macmillan Publishers Limited
4 Little Essex Street London WC2R 3LF
and Basingstoke
Associated companies in Auckland, Delhi, Dublin, Gaborone,
Hamburg, Harare, Hong Kong, Johannesburg, Kuala Lumpur,
Lagos, Manzini, Melbourne, Mexico City, Nairobi, New York,
Singapore and Tokyo

British Library Cataloguing in Publication Data
Freedom of information . . . freedom of the
    individual.——(Days of decision).
    1. Civil rights——Great Britain
    I. Neuberger, Julia   II. Series
    323.4′0941   JN906

ISBN 0-333-44771-9

Typeset by Columns of Reading
Printed by Richard Clay plc, Bungay, Suffolk

Contents

Introduction

Until recently the debate about freedom of information and freedom of the individual was regarded by the majority of the population as 'boring', incomprehensible or irrelevant. Suddenly, however, the Right to Know has become a national issue. Such disparate issues as the Zircon Spy Satellite Affair, the Wright case in Australia, the Tamil refugees, and the seventeen year-old mentally handicapped girl in Sunderland whom the Appeal Court judges ruled was to be sterilised, have caused enormous public concern about secrecy, the politicisation of the civil service and intelligence agencies, the power of the state, the role of the judges and the lack of Parliamentary power in various areas of national life. Discussion about a possible Bill of Rights and Freedom of Information Act is now high on the political agenda.

Although a Bill of Rights would protect specific human rights of the individual against the State or giant corporations, whereas a Freedom of Information Act would be more concerned with official secrecy, both issues are inextricably bound together in philosophical terms and both are addressed in this volume. Professor Michael Zander argues for and Simon Lee against a Bill of Rights; Clive Ponting argues in favour of a Freedom of Information Act, whilst John Ranelagh sees value in official secrecy. All four writers have made important contributions to a debate that affects all our futures: where does power lie and how can the individual achieve redress of grievance?

Julia Neuberger

Secrecy and Freedom of Information

Clive Ponting

Britain is the most secretive nation this side of the Iron Curtain. The tradition of British government is that it is conducted by a small group of insiders – ministers and senior civil servants – and the public should be involved only when the insiders judge that it is the best time to tell it what has been decided. The idea of an informed and extensive public debate before decisions are reached is deeply alien to the British political system. The campaign for a Freedom of Information Act seeks to change that tradition and as a consequence bring about a significant redistribution of power in favour of the ordinary citizen. This is why those in power are opposed to such a change.

Secrecy is a fundamental part of the way British government works, the cement which holds the current system together. It is convenient for those in power because it enables them to take decisions well away from the glare of publicity, to ignore arguments which they find inconvenient and to suppress information that would be embarrassing. When the time has come to announce a decision, a government is able to present facts and figures in a way that supports what it has already decided to do, free from the fear that the full facts will be available. Through a wall of secrecy government propaganda is pumped, masquerading as information.

Excessive secrecy damages the democratic process and leads to poor decision-taking, because ministers and bureaucrats become isolated from the real world. Secrecy means that both individuals and pressure groups are unable to gain access to information that would enable them to challenge what has been decided in Whitehall. By opening up this whole process, freedom of information would lead to an improvement both in the way decisions are taken and in the quality of those decisions.

The Official Secrets Act

At the heart of government secrecy in Britain lies the Official Secrets Act, in particular its Section 2. Everybody joining the Civil Service has to 'sign' the Official Secrets Act whether they are a top mandarin in Whitehall, a gardener at Hampton Court Palace or a cleaner. This is because Section 2 covers every single piece of information in Whitehall, from the most mundane (the number of paperclips ordered or the menu in the canteen) to the most important (the design of nuclear weapons or the next Budget), in exactly the same way. Section 1 of the Act deals with spying, and its use has been relatively uncontroversial. The trials which have roused controversy have involved the 'catch-all' provisions of Section 2 and its blanket protection of every item of information inside Whitehall. How did such an all-embracing piece of legislation come to be passed?

The Official Secrets Act was enacted in 1911, but the crucial decisions were taken a few years before amid great secrecy. Ministers and senior officials felt that they did not have enough powers to control the information available to the press, but they realised that to seek to impose censorship would be unpopular and perhaps impossible. So they decided to prepare the legislation and wait for a suitable occasion, such as a war scare, and then ask for the Bill to be passed rapidly through Parliament. The opportunity came in 1911 during the Agadir crisis, when war between Germany and Britain loomed. The Bill went through all its stages in the House of Commons in just forty minutes with no substantive debate and not a single mention of Section 2. The government deliberately gave the impression that the Bill was concerned only with espionage, although it knew full well that its provisions were far wider. The minister concerned, Colonel Seely, gave this assurance: 'The actual change in the law is slight, and it is perfectly true to say that none of His Majesty's loyal subjects run the least risk whatever of having their liberties infringed in any degree or particular.' The number of people prosecuted under the Act in the last seventy-five years, and the way the Act has been used, have shown such assurances to be worthless.

Almost from the start, the Act was used not to protect genuine military and diplomatic secrets but to prevent embarrassment to the authorities. In the 1920s a governor of Pentonville prison was found guilty of publishing in a London evening newspaper the last-minute confessions of a condemned murderer. In the early 1930s the well-known author Compton Mackenzie was prosecuted for attempting to publish his war memoirs about the Gallipoli campaign. Later in the decade the authorities threatened to prosecute Duncan Sandys MP for revealing deficiencies in the air defences around London which he had discovered as an officer in the Territorial Army. After a major parliamentary row and inquiry, the proceedings were dropped.

One of the most significant cases after the war came in 1971 when Jonathan Aitken, now a Tory MP, the editor of the *Sunday Telegraph*, and his newspaper were prosecuted for publishing a semi-official report about the Nigerian civil war. What embarrassed the government was the fact that the report showed that assurances given to Parliament about the supply of weapons by Britain to the Federal government were not correct. All the defendants were acquitted. Six years later came the 'ABC' trial, named after the three defendants Aubrey, Berry and Campbell. Berry was an ex-soldier who had been interviewed by two journalists about the activities of GCHQ, the government communications headquarters at Cheltenham, which the government was then trying to pretend did not engage in code-breaking (a fact which it has since admitted). After a highly controversial trial, in which nearly all the charges had to be dropped by the prosecution on the instructions of the judge, the defendants were found guilty but were not given jail sentences.

In 1984 Sarah Tisdall, a clerk in the Foreign Office, was charged after she had sent two documents to the *Guardian* about the arrival of United States cruise missiles in Britain. She decided to plead guilty and was sentenced to six months' imprisonment − a sentence that met with almost universal condemnation. The next year there was my own trial at the Old Bailey after I had sent two Ministry of Defence documents to the Labour MP Tam Dalyell. The documents revealed that there had been a two-year-long systematic cover-up by the government of the events surrounding the sinking of the Argentinian cruiser *General Belgrano* during the Falklands conflict. After a trial in which the judge attempted to direct the jury to convict me, I was unanimously found not guilty.

It is now generally accepted that Section 2 of the Official Secrets Act is thoroughly discredited and unusable, yet it has still not been replaced. How does the Act work and what are its provisions? The section is long and complicated even by legal standards; it has been calculated that it creates over two thousand different offences. In essence Section 2 makes the communication of any item of official information to an 'unauthorised person' a criminal offence punishable by up to two years in prison. The information does not have to be classified as 'secret' or 'confidential' and it need not affect national security. Just as it is an offence to communicate the information, it is also an offence under Section 2(2) to receive official information in contravention of the Act. However, it is interesting that in both Sarah Tisdall's case and my own neither the *Guardian* nor Tam Dalyell was charged with an offence.

Since the Act is so all-embracing it is inevitably breached thousands of times every day. Every civil servant who goes home after work and tells their wife or husband what they did at the office during the day is committing a criminal offence. The absurd lengths to which the Act can be taken are best illustrated by the case that was going through the courts behind mine in 1985. A senior Home Office official was charged under Section 2 with communicating information to another civil servant in the Home Office but one who was not authorised to receive the information. The case was hurriedly dropped a few days after my acquittal.

If the law is broken so frequently, why is it that the criminal courts are not clogged up with erring civil servants? The answer lies in a peculiar British institution: the Attorney-General, who controls all prosecutions under the Official Secrets Act. The peculiarity lies in the theory that he is supposed to wear two hats at the same time; he must carry out two separate roles and never confuse the two functions. On the one hand he is supposed to be the government's independent legal adviser, able to reach a completely unbiased decision about the 'public interest' in bringing any prosecution. On the other hand he is also a government minister, appointed by the Prime Minister and a member of the governing party. In practice what happens is that the two supposedly independent roles have become hopelessly intertwined, and the definition of the 'public interest' is nearly always identical with the interests of the government. The Attorney-General is thus in a position to ensure that no prosecution seen as potentially damaging to the government will be brought.

Defences Against Prosecution

Once proceedings have been taken, there are only two possible defences that can be made under the Act. A defendant can argue that the communication of information was 'authorised' or that it was 'in the interests of the state'. The scope for mounting a defence case adopting either of these approaches is limited.

It is extremely difficult for the defendant to demonstrate 'authorisation', to show that the communication was in some way 'official'. There are no clearly laid down rules and regulations. It is a question of custom and practice, much of which is kept deliberately obscure. In this way the provisions of the Official Secrets Act and the undefined concept of authorisation underlie the way much information gets into the public domain in Britain.

Because ministers are at the top of the chain of command they are able to 'authorise' themselves to release any information they like, including that classified 'secret' or 'confidential'. This they do regularly to journalists in order to get the stories they want into the press. Political correspondents regularly carry stories saying that 'senior Cabinet ministers take the view that . . .', together with detailed accounts of what took place in Cabinet meetings. In practice senior civil servants have a great deal of discretion in what they say to the press and are virtually in a position to authorise themselves to give out stories. Many other examples of impromptu 'self-authorisation' could be cited. In the Ministry of Defence during any review of defence spending the Chiefs of Staff always felt free to brief the military correspondents about what was happening in an attempt to avoid the worst of the cuts – even going so far on occasions as to criticise the government. No prosecution followed. Because they held senior posts it was practically impossible for them to be sacked. Thus there is a continual stream of stories from Whitehall which may seem like 'leaks', but because they are 'authorised' they come into the category of 'briefings'. Ministers spend a great deal of their time informally briefing the media, retailing political gossip or even stories against their Cabinet colleagues, as the Westland affair demonstrated.

The concept of 'authorisation' lies at the heart of the main conduit for the flow of information from Whitehall to the media: the justly criticised 'lobby' system. The lobby started in the late nineteenth century as a group of journalists who gathered in the lobby of the House of Commons, where they would pick up political gossip from politicians. It has now evolved into a complex system of formal briefings for the media. The rule of the lobby is that officially none of the conversations take place, and the remarks made by politicians cannot be attributed to them by name. The government runs a highly organised set of briefings throughout the week. Every weekday at 11 a.m. the Prime Minister's Press Secretary talks to the provincial daily papers and at 4 p.m. to the London daily papers, giving them all the stories that No. 10 Downing Street wants to slip into the press. On Thursday afternoons the Leader of the House of Commons holds a briefing mainly to say what went on at the Cabinet meeting that morning. On Friday afternoons there is a special briefing for the Sunday papers for the stories Whitehall wants planted at that time. In addition each Whitehall department is covered by a team of specialist correspondents who receive weekly briefings on lobby terms.

The lobby has continued because both sides benefit from the current arrangements. The politicians are able to get the stories they want into the media, perhaps revealing their colleagues in a less than flattering light, without the fear that their remarks will be attributed to them by name. In the same way civil servants have been used to criticise the opposition parties and their fitness to govern, again without fear of exposing the source. At the same time the journalists get their story and appear to be in the know in terms of political gossip. But this process is far removed from investigative journalism, because the lobby correspondents are content to accept the stories at face value and do not criticise what they are told. The lobby is therefore bad journalism and bad for the flow of information to the public. The whole cynical nature of the system was well summed up by Sir Robert Armstrong, Secretary to the Cabinet, when he described its aims as 'to seek to influence opinion without accepting responsibility'. The basis for all this activity is the Official Secrets Act and the concept of 'authorisation'.

The other defence to a charge under Section 2 of the Act – that the communication of information was 'in the interests of the state' – was first deployed as a defence in my own trial at the Old Bailey. There we argued that Parliament was part of the state in this country and that it must therefore be a fundamental interest that it is told the truth. Indeed the whole system of British democracy would break down if ministers were able to lie to Parliament with impunity; they would no longer be accountable for their actions and could do whatever they liked. We called as witnesses the main expert on constitutional law in the country, Professor Wade, and a senior ex-Cabinet minister, Merlyn Rees, to testify to the jury that this was indeed the case. However, the judge took the view that the jury should not be asked to consider what the interests of the state might be. Instead he ruled in Orwellian fashion that the interests of the state were the same as the interests of the government of the day. In other words, if the government decided that it was in its short-term political interests to withhold information from Parliament or to tell lies, then it was by definition in the interests of the state that it should do so. Although the jury took no notice of this ruling and unanimously acquitted me, the legal ruling still remains. The current Attorney-General, Sir Michael Havers, has stated officially that he agrees with the view of the judge. If this is really what the Official Secrets Act says, then it is indeed time it was repealed as a danger to democracy.

Other Areas of Secrecy

So far the discussion has been about central government and the operation of the Official Secrets Act, but secrecy in Britain extends to every area of life. Official secrecy covers all aspects of government, including advisory committees that do not comprise civil servants. For example, people who serve on committees investigating the number of additives in food are covered by the Official Secrets Act so that the information does not reach the public. There is a widespread tendency to use secrecy and the threat of the criminal law not to protect genuine secrets but to guard against political embarrassment. In 1985 the *Guardian* was given a leaked paper from the Department of Health and Social Security showing that ministers intended to cut £120 million from the poorest when they had given a public pledge that there would be no cash cuts. What is interesting is that the document was classified 'secret'. The official definition of a secret document is that its release would cause 'serious injury to the interests of the nation'. Now, it is obvious that a paper about social security payments cannot fall into such a category, but there is no doubt that it might cause serious injury to the interests of some government ministers. In other words, security was being used to protect them from political embarrassment.

Apart from the Official Secrets Act there are more than a hundred different statutes that make the disclosure of information a criminal offence. A good example of the overriding priority given to secrecy in Britain is the rules governing the pollution of rivers by industrial companies. If a firm were breaching the relatively generous limits on waste discharges into rivers it might, if found guilty, be fined a small amount. However, if an inspector who discovered this fact made the information public he could face up to three months in jail. Not just matters of high policy are involved, but everyday matters affecting every individual. If you are buying a car and would like to see the official statistics showing which cars have failed government safety tests, you cannot, because it is an official secret. If you are buying a gas cooker and would like to know the results of government safety tests, you cannot, because this, too, is an official secret. If you are worried by the local chemical factory and would like to know what dangerous chemicals are stored there, you will not be able to find out, because the government agency that collects such information treats it as an official secret. There was much justified criticism of the Soviet government for its unwillingness to release information about the Chernobyl nuclear disaster; yet it took the British government *twenty-six years* to admit the full extent of the damage caused by the Windscale fire in 1957 and the highly dangerous radioactive elements released into the atmosphere.

In area after area we come up against the same obsession with secrecy. One of the most important concerns the personal records kept on individuals by a whole range of bodies and individuals including local authority housing departments, doctors, dentists, schools and education and social service departments. It is almost invariably the practice that individuals are not allowed access to these files even simply to check whether there are any inaccuracies. The result is predictable. When the files are examined they are found to contain wrong information and even disparaging remarks about the individuals concerned which can have profound effects on their lives – influencing, for example, the education of their children, the allocation of council housing or their treatment by doctors.

Everywhere the picture is the same. When a choice has to be made, a decision is taken in favour of secrecy and in favour of the institution holding the information. The right of the public to know information of crucial importance and the right of the individual to be told what facts are being held about him or her are disregarded. Secrecy is the British disease, but something can be done to remedy the situation and to make sure that the individual and the public obtain the rights to which they are entitled.

Freedom of Information

The first stage of the process would be to reform Section 2 of the Official Secrets Act. This has long been recommended but not implemented. In 1971 the Heath government set up a committee of inquiry under Lord Franks to investigate the operation of Section 2. The Franks Report was a damning indictment of the existing law:

> We found Section 2 a mess. Its scope is enormously wide. Any law which impinges on the freedom of information in a democracy should be much more tightly drawn. A catch-all provision is saved from absurdity in operation only by the sparing exercise of the

Attorney-General's discretion, and the inevitably selective way in which it is exercised gives rise to considerable
unease. The drafting and interpretation of the Section
are obscure. People are not sure what it means, or how it
operates in practice, or what kind of actions involve real
risk of prosecution under it.

The Franks Committee recommended that in future the
criminal law should deal only with the disclosure of information classified 'secret' and above. This is the obvious solution
that needs to be implemented in any reform of Section 2,
so that only those crucially important items of military and
diplomatic information that need to be protected are covered
by criminal sanctions. Any civil servant who disclosed
without authorisation information classified less than 'secret'
could still be dismissed, so there would still be considerable
protection for all government information.

Reform of the Official Secrets Act, however, desirable as
that would be in itself, would not alone increase the flow of
information available to the ordinary citizen. In order to
achieve this it is necessary to introduce a Freedom of
Information Act to give individuals access to government
information as of right. How would such an Act work? In
practice its operation would be relatively simple. Every
government department would be required to keep a register
of all its files and documents, which anybody would be able to
inspect without having to give their reasons. The department
would be legally obliged to produce any paper asked for
within a specified period, on payment of a small fee to cover
the administrative costs involved. The Act would lay down the
principle that documents were available to the public
except in a number of carefully defined and limited circumstances. Sensitive military and diplomatic information would
be excepted, but the general presumption of the legislation
would be that files would be made available unless the
government department could show good reason why they
should not. Where access was refused it would be necessary
to have an appeal procedure to an independent tribunal in

order to stop the government acting as both judge and jury on whether information should be released.

The tribunal would have powers to examine any document that the government refused to make public; if it decided that the papers fell within the provisions of the Act, it would have the power to order their release. Inevitably appointments to the tribunal will be made by the government and that is why it is so important that its powers are clearly defined in the Freedom of Information Act to ensure that it is able to function effectively. It should also have to make an annual report to Parliament to increase its accountability in the same way as the Ombudsman does already.

Freedom of information would therefore reverse the current situation. At present it is assumed that all government information is private and nothing to do with the ordinary individual except when the government decides that it would be to its own advantage to release it. Under a Freedom of Information Act the presumption would be that the information should be made available unless the government can show good reason why it should not. That is a fundamental difference in approach that to most people inside Whitehall would seem revolutionary.

In fact it is not revolutionary at all. Britain is now almost the only Western democracy without some form of freedom of information legislation. The practice in Sweden goes back to the end of the eighteenth century and in the other Scandinavian countries to the mid-nineteenth century. One of the most fundamental measures was introduced in the United States in the 1960s and further extended a decade ago. Freedom of information laws were recently introduced in both France and West Germany. It is often argued in Britain that the idea of freedom of information is unnecessary and alien to Westminster-style democracy, where ministers are accountable to the House of Commons. Such an argument ignores the fact that freedom of information has in recent years successfully operated in Canada, Australia and New Zealand, which all have political systems modelled on Westminster.

It is worth examining just how accountable ministers are to Parliament before freedom of information is dismissed as unnecessary. At first glance the picture would seem to be reassuring. Ministers regularly have to face questioning in the House of Commons; there are frequent topical debates, and select committees investigate government policy, summoning witnesses and looking out for waste and inefficiency. In practice none of these controls is particularly effective. The crucial factor is the domination of the House of Commons by the governing party. Back-bench MPs rely on the party for promotion and preferment and, unlike Senators and Congressmen in the United States, they do not have independent power-bases that would enable them to challenge the administration. The government can therefore rely on the support of its back-benchers and can usually pass any legislation it likes. It is a very rare event indeed for a government to lose the support of its own followers over any important issue. Serious criticism of the government is largely left to the opposition parties, where it can more easily be dismissed as mere point-scoring and party-political carping.

Question time is not an effective way of controlling the government. Each MP is limited to just one supplementary question, and the minister can normally evade any detailed scrutiny. If questions do stray into difficult areas there are plenty of ways in which a minister can avoid having to reveal embarrassing facts. The information may be withheld on the grounds that it is 'not readily available' or 'not available except at disproportionate cost' (i.e. more than £250), or a minister can reply that 'it is not our practice to reveal such information'. Another major constraint is that ordinary MPs are almost entirely lacking in support. They do not have the vast number of research assistants available to United States legislators – they are lucky if they have even one – and Parliament itself has very few staff who can help MPs. The whole contest between the government and Parliament is therefore unequal, and for those in power parliamentary debate is often no more than an irritating accompaniment to decisions that have already been taken.

Similarly the select committees that seem to be so powerful turn out on closer examination to be toothless tigers. The main reason is that the government has a majority of MPs on every committee. So once again criticism remains muted. The committees can do some useful work in uncontroversial areas, but when an issue of major political importance arises the majority of MPs side with the government and seek to restrict the committee's investigations and ensure that its report is emasculated. Under the present system the government is not accountable to Parliament in any meaningful sense, and it is not therefore possible to sustain the argument that this form of accountability is a substitute for freedom of information laws. On the contrary, such legislation would improve the work of Parliament by providing it with more facts with which to scrutinise the operations of government.

While in opposition, politicians often proclaim the benefits that freedom of information would bring, but the truth of the old adage 'information is power' is demonstrated when they take office. In government they see the benefits of the existing system and relish their ability to deny the opposition parties information which could be used to criticise them. In this attitude they are strongly supported by the Civil Service, which has no interest in improving the ability of Parliament to ask awkward questions or in opening up the channels of communication to ministers which it controls so tightly at present. Thus over the last fifteen years there has been the spectacle of politicians advocating reform of Section 2 of the Official Secrets Act and even the introduction of freedom of information legislation when in opposition, but rapidly losing interest and failing to make any changes once in power.

In 1970 the Heath government was pledged to end unnecessary secrecy and set up the Franks Committee to report on reform of Section 2. It then spent the next two years looking at the report but did nothing to implement it. In 1974 Labour was pledged to reform Section 2 and introduce freedom of information. Over the next four years legislation to amend Section 2 was twice promised in a Queen's Speech, and there were also a White Paper and a Green Paper; but absolutely nothing was achieved. In opposition the Tories felt free to flay the government for its inability to get rid of Section 2. In one debate Leon Brittan said: 'That Section of the Act is simply indefensible yet it is still there. Why is that? It is still there, in spite of the Government's assurances, because they have not had the courage to fight and overcome the strenuous rearguard action mounted in the more obscurantist corners of Whitehall.'

A few years later Leon Brittan was to be Home Secretary, responsible for the Official Secrets Act. He did nothing to initiate any reform. There was, however, one member of the opposition who did not share these views, and that was Margaret Thatcher when Leader of the Opposition. During a visit to the United States she was asked whether Britain had anything to learn from the much more open system of government operating there. She gave a remarkable reply: 'Nothing at all; our system is much more open than the American one. The Official Secrets Act should be reformed but only to make some of its provisions against the unauthorised disclosure of information stronger, not weaker.'

On gaining office in 1979 this is exactly what the Tory government proceeded to do. In the autumn of that year it introduced a Bill interestingly entitled the Protection of Official Information Bill. This partly implemented recommendations of the Franks Committee. In introducing the Bill in the House of Lords, the Lord Chancellor, Lord Hailsham, was still able to use the rhetoric of the opposition when speaking about Section 2: 'Are we to leave on the statute book a section which is really manifestly intolerable because it is unjust and anachronistic; and if tolerable at all, is tolerable only because it is unenforceable and unenforced and therefore brings the law into disrepute?' Although it might not seem possible to make the existing situation worse, this is exactly what the government proposals would have done. Use of the criminal law would have been restricted to information classified 'secret' or higher, as the Franks Committee had recommended, but a certificate signed by a minister would have been conclusive proof in a court that the document was correctly classified. Since there would be no defence to a charge under the new Act if the disclosure were unauthorised, the ministerial certificate would have been the same as a conviction.

However, the 1979 Bill went even further in restricting the flow of information and the right to comment. No public discussion of some matters would have been legal. It would, for example, have become a criminal offence even to mention the existence of either MI5 or MI6 or the fact that telephone tapping took place in Britain. Not only that: it would have been a criminal offence to repeat information about MI5 or MI6 that was already publicly available. Such an illiberal Bill caused a storm of protest. When it became clear that under its provisions the book that had just unmasked Anthony Blunt as a Soviet spy could not have been published, the government was forced to withdraw the measure. It then decided to do nothing more to reform the Official Secrets Act; indeed, the Attorney-General, Sir Michael Havers, has used the Act on more occasions than any of his predecessors.

The present government has done nothing in the last eight years to deal with the problem of secrecy. On the contrary, it has taken many steps to increase the amount of secrecy and restrict the right to comment – for example, in gagging the *Guardian* and *Observer* newspapers over the Peter Wright trial in Australia. Nevertheless the issue of secrecy remains on the political agenda. Both the Labour Party and the Alliance are pledged to reform Section 2 and to introduce a Freedom of Information Act if they gain power at the next election. We have seen that politicians in the past have said one thing in opposition and done nothing when in power. Will it be any different this time? One of the reasons for thinking that things may change is the existence of a vigorous pressure group: the Campaign for Freedom of Information, which includes representatives from all political parties and other groups such as the Civil Service trade unions. The campaign has already secured firm commitments to legislate from all the leaders of the opposition parties and has sponsored Bills in Parliament to open up the proceedings of local councils. It is currently sponsoring another Bill to secure access to personal files. The main aim of the campaign is to keep the issue high on the political agenda until the general election and then to ensure that commitments are honoured.

Conclusion

The issue of freedom of information needs to be near the top of the political agenda. Although the condition of the economy, unemployment, law and order and defence are always going to be bigger electoral issues, secrecy and access to information are an area where fundamental reform is needed. Too often we have seen governments attempting to change either society or the economy but making no effort to alter how British government operates or how individuals can affect decision-taking. Not surprisingly, many government initiatives have failed because of poorly thought out policies which have been subject to far too little discussion and analysis in public beforehand, being instead based on inadequate work carried out in secret in Whitehall involving just a small group of poorly trained civil servants and ministers. The improvement in the quality of British government that is so urgently needed will not be achieved within the current structure. Freedom of information is not a 'left–right' issue but one that affects all governments. As Sir John Hoskyns, head of the policy unit inside No. 10 for Margaret Thatcher, has said: 'Open government is not a fashionable option but a precondition for any serious attempt to solve Britain's underlying problems. The Official Secrets Act, by hiding peacetime fiascos as though they were military disasters, protects Ministers and officials from embarrassment.'

Freedom of information is also about the quality of democracy. It raises the question of whether democracy is simply a matter of putting a cross on a ballot paper once every four or five years, and then leaving a small group of some one hundred politicians and top civil servants to govern the nation and occasionally tell the rest of us what they are doing by releasing some information in support of their decisions. With freedom of information we could have a much better-informed democracy in which pressure groups and individuals would be able to question more effectively what is done in their name and influence decisions before they are made. Any such change would require a fundamental shift in attitude among politicians and civil servants and the introduction of a much more participatory style of government. It would also mean a great many changes in the way the media operate, away from the easy regurgitation of the lobby briefing and the government hand-out and towards a more investigative approach. All of this would provide a much needed shake-up and a potentially healthy stimulus for democracy, government, the media and British society as a whole.

The extent to which the results would be of benefit would depend on what use could be made of information freed under the Act. Amassing large amounts of material is not in itself a fruitful occupation. What is it all for? Achieving freedom of information, however vital, is only part of the story. The quality of life and government in Britain beyond a Freedom of Information Act would depend on the mechanisms for holding the government and the bureaucracy to account. Only when government is not only more open but also more accountable will the real benefits of freedom of information begin to be seen.

Secrets, Supervision and Information

John Ranelagh

Today there is increasing interest in the nature of secrecy and secrets in Britain. There are two reasons for this. First, people suspect that the officials of secrecy operate an invisible, unelected government that subverts democracy. Second, people suspect that secrecy hides inefficiency.

The first reason is not based on fact. It is based on fear and indicates a subconscious awareness that as individuals we are not in control of our own destinies. Official secrecy is the convenient focus for this fear. The fact is that since 1945 we have become far more aware of the complexities and supranational connections that determine our possibilities, and of the speed at which things happen. Technological advances of all descriptions have spread this awareness. Six years after the first atom bomb, we had Sakharov's improved hydrogen bomb. Six years after that, the first satellite was in space. Twenty-four years after the end of the Second World War, astronauts were on the moon. Since 1970 we have experienced domestic computers and video-cassette machines. Since 1980 direct-dial cellular telephones and direct broadcasting by satellite have been introduced. The speed of change has challenged certainties and encouraged us to question what is termed secret, because secrecy is seen among other things as the source of change and of shock.

The Need for Secrecy in Security Matters

There is clearly a core of secrecy necessary for any state to conduct its business. This area involves military and intelligence secrets, a certain amount of strategic economic policy, policing, the details of foreign policy and diplomacy, and prison security. Nations essentially behave in the same way as home-owners who keep the secrets of their burglar alarm systems from strangers. Understanding the need for self-protection, a practical public does in fact endorse the existence of special groups with special powers in the form of élite democratic bodies such as the Special Air Service, with its operations against terrorists in Northern Ireland or at the Iranian Embassy in London. In effect, the public gives certain information the status of democratically sanctioned secrets. People want an economy of confidence; they do not want to agonise all the time with the elected government over what to do. There was no public outcry over the sinking of the *Belgrano* during the Falklands war, and there was no flood of letters to MPs or massed protests in Parliament Square subsequently, despite the best efforts of Tam Dalyell and Clive Ponting. People in general did not want to know or were not particularly concerned that the sinking of the *Belgrano* took place as the cruiser was sailing back to port and was thus somehow less of a military threat. Clearly, it is impossible for the democratic system to function in any other way. A democracy would collapse under the weight of full disclosure accompanied by debate; decision-making would be paralysed.

For a democracy to function, there has to be some degree of public approval. But most ordinary citizens never ask for more than a general understanding of how democracy protects itself. Technical secrets – such as those concerning the specifications of weapons, the names of secret agents or military orders of battle, or the secrets allies entrust to one another – need to be kept until out of date, and this people accept. People do not want to know the gory details of battle nor to have a specific understanding of how an 'anti-personnel mine' tears a person apart. People also accept the need for secrecy for negotiating purposes. No country can deal with others on matters of national security without withholding vital information that, if known, could threaten its very existence.

Other secrets, however, even if people do not actually want to know them, should not be kept. People should know, for example, the economic agreements made by government with other countries and with private firms and banks. They should know about government deals of all sorts, from the basis upon which a tank is declared surplus and sold off, to the land-purchasing plans of local councils. They should know if torture and murder are being committed by police or military officers. And even if there is no public outcry when such matters are revealed, it is an essential part of the democratic responsibility that people should know them.

The Nature of Secrecy

The 1911 Official Secrets Act, in force (with changes) today, provides the statutory umbrella for state secrecy in the United Kingdom. It is underwritten by the interpretation of secrecy intensified by the experience of two world wars, and the result is comprehensive and suffocating, an invitation to systematic violation. Any law that makes such a large invitation leads to consistent hypocrisy in practice. We also have a general rule that official records are not released until twenty-five years have passed. This time period can be infinitely extended by the head of the Civil Service. For example, some records of administration in Ireland, over a century old, are still kept secret. Britain has no Freedom of Information Act. It has a Security Commission within the Civil Service that can investigate the security services but only on the instruction of the Prime Minister. It has the D-notice system whereby news stories considered revealing of official secrets can be censored and banned by a Civil Service committee. It has a voluntary lobby system in which unattri-butable briefings are given to chosen journalists by govern-ment press officers, senior civil servants and ministers, although the lobby system is now beginning to break down.

Two national newspapers, the *Independent* and the *Guardian*, and the Liberal and Social Democrat parties have withdrawn from it.

By contrast, secrecy in the United States occupies only a small area within government. A Freedom of Information Act guarantees people the means to discover government information of most sorts, from telephone tapping by the Federal Bureau of Investigation to the negotiating papers of trade delegations. There is no Official Secrets Act in the USA, and there have never been D-notices or lobby arrangements. The Central Intelligence Agency, the USA's principal secret service, even has a press office and is supervised by eight congressional committees. However, as I will go on to argue, the political cultures of Britain and the United States are entirely different, and therefore it is not simply a question of introducing US-style legislation or increasing the powers of privileged committees to supervise government secrecy in Britain. What is necessary is to make vastly more information about decision-making in Britain public.

Having kept decision-making secret for decades, we have ended up treating each other like children. Secrets have become tokens of status and power in the same way that parents establish adulthood by keeping things from children. As you grow up, you are told, more will be revealed. But for the last seventy years Britain has visibly been in decline, and the secrets of government have grown and been impenetrable to all but a handful of politicians and civil servants. This has fuelled the feeling that there would not be so many secrets if something discreditable were not involved.

If we correlate our system of secrecy with our decline, we face the inescapable fact that our system of decision-making has not worked well. Secrecy and inefficiency have gone hand in hand and this is the true reason why we should be concerned about secrecy and the availability of information. We cannot assume that government and the Civil Service will always do their best or know best what to do; we should not allow the very small number of people who have made a lifetime commitment to politics to continue to select talent and deploy the nation's resources without far more information, debate and challenge.

Differences of Political Culture

The basis of secrecy in each country lies in the full nature of the state. In the democracies, while there are some essential similarities – regular elections, the secret ballot, the rule of law, accountability, the supremacy of parliament, the public freedom to question, to criticise and to disagree – there are also major differences which relate to the political cultures of each country, making comparisons far more complicated than is often assumed by those who draw them.

Frustration is the hallmark of secrecy and the exercise of power in the United States. This is because of the ordinary condition of any constitutional government: the constitution. By setting up a tripartite nexus of checks and balances between the legislature, the judiciary and the executive, the founding fathers of the American revolution guaranteed rivalry and restriction. They did so consciously, seeing in the resulting emotions a powerful and natural opposition to the United States ever developing an overweening government. In the fiercely competitive democratic arena of US politics, as a consequence, power is associated with publicity.

Consensus is the British hallmark. Britain does not have a written constitution. There are no built-in checks and balances. There is instead an evolution of political licence. Precedence and the rule of law condition developments. The government's freedom of action lies in whatever perceptions there may be about normal political behaviour within the context of the country's resources at any time. Power in Britain is associated with secrecy. Thus a generation ago Mr (now Sir) Robin Day shocked people when he asked the Prime Minister on television a question about his plans for a Cabinet shuffle. Today, speculation on Cabinet shuffles is commonplace. The fact that Prime Ministers can no longer shuffle Cabinet ministers without public speculation represents a reduction of their power and an increase in the power of the media. And it is reasonable to presume, further, that the consensus of public speculation about who should be shuffled and why has become a political factor that Prime Ministers must take into account as they plan changes, and not simply after they have made them.

Britain's political culture has not developed from a revolutionary determination, but from a monarchical (as opposed to a democratic) European sensibility that, historically, has recognised the need to accommodate democratic impulses. Not until the British Nationality Act 1981, which came into force on 1 January 1983, for example, was there such a condition as a 'British citizen'. Until then, being British was a gift of the Crown. Britons – and anyone else the government determined – were only 'subjects of the Crown' and had no right to a passport or, indeed, residence in the United Kingdom. 'The main reason why it was necessary to replace the existing law', explained the Home Secretary to Parliament, 'was quite simply that the citizenship created by the British Nationality Act, 1948, had long since ceased to give any clear indication of who had the right to enter the United Kingdom. Citizenship and right of abode, which ought to be related, had over the years parted company from each other.' The British Governor-General's dismissal of Gough Whitlam's administration in Australia in 1975 was another example of the monarchical core of British political culture. The dismissal did not occur after an election, a referendum or a parliamentary vote of no confidence. It took place without public debate. The Governor-General was exercising royal and not parliamentary power. Such an action would be impossible in the United States.

In 1985 and 1986 two affairs involving government secrets demonstrated in a mundane way the operating differences between the European and American sensibilities. The sinking of the *Rainbow Warrior* saw no surge of horror in French public opinion. The French government did not fall. Yet two

French secret service officers had sunk a ship and killed a man in the harbour of a friendly country. The second affair was when the British Cabinet Secretary, Sir Robert Armstrong, admitted in an Australian court that he was 'economical with the truth'. He returned to London and discreet eminence. In the United States, in both cases, there would have been an outcry.

Culturally and institutionally the European countries and the United States are very different. In Britain we tend to obscure this fact by assuming that because English is the common language the two countries have a natural understanding of each other. American government is vastly more individualist than European, and much more pressure can be brought to bear on it by a single misfortune. One American held hostage by terrorists in the Lebanon really does distress the American people and the US government. The same cannot be said for Britain and France.

The degree to which power is focused in Britain has no parallel in the United States. The USA has two proud, fiercely independent houses of Congress. The courts are powerful, and so is the Presidency. The USA has many magnetising cities and centres of achievement. It has no national newspapers. There is no mystique of the state in the USA. In Britain, by contrast, the focus is on the Prime Minister, the Civil Service, the House of Commons and London. Parliament is not independent of the government; the purpose of parliamentary majorities is to support the government. In the USA the legislature's independence is a constitutional requirement.

These differences mean that the US experience of congressional supervision of the secret activities of government, and the amount of public disclosure ensured by congressional inquiry, cannot be simply translated to Britain.

Would Supervision Work?

Supervision of the secret services in the United States is the responsibility of congressional committees. Such a function, undertaken by either the House of Commons or the House of Lords, or a combination of both, would not work in the British system. It would be impossible, given the purpose of parliamentary majorities in Britain, to obtain a parliamentary committee that would speak with the voice of the House of Commons. If a committee were to have a degree of power comparable to a congressional committee in the USA, Parliament would have to accept the existence of a power equal to its own and outside its control. It is inconceivable in the British system for a parliamentary committee genuinely to be able to invigilate and rebuke a Prime Minister. For this to happen would require a revolutionary dispersal of power that would result in governments falling whenever a rebuke was delivered, because each rebuke, in such circumstances, would be the equivalent of a parliamentary vote of no confidence. The government is subordinate to Parliament, and the crucial power relationship in Britain lies in the government's control of its parliamentary majority. If a committee had real power – the power to rebuke and penalise – the government would be subordinate to it rather than to Parliament.

Even the Public Accounts Committee, the most important parliamentary committee, has little real power. Its achievements lie in its debates with the Civil Service and in the refinement of legislation. It is a way for back-benchers to let off steam, and its status indicates little more than a decent respect for public opinion. When, in January 1987, it emerged that the committee might have been misled four years earlier about expenditure on a spy satellite, it had no power to rebuke the minister and officials concerned.

If a supervisory committee with real power was to be established composed of the great and the good – Privy Councillors, academics, retired civil servants and military people, and captains of finance and industry – the question would be raised by parliamentarians why they should have powers of no confidence over the elected government. And the answer would be to subject such a committee to Parliament, and then the government majority would operate to emasculate, censor, deny and suppress. If such a committee were to be established in the House of Lords, the convention of the last 150 years that the Lords cannot overthrow a government based in the House of Commons would operate. A Lords committee, therefore, would be equally ineffective.

It is impossible to see how, in the British system, the power of supervision can be distributed away from the Prime Minister and Cabinet. To distribute this power would be disruptive and counter-productive. It would give back-benchers an alternative route to power and would disperse party authority. Either the government would effectively control appointments to committees and thereby ensure that no parliamentary committee ever seriously challenged it (as is the case today), or the committees would have to find some mechanism for appointing themselves. In this latter case, there would then develop a new process of the confirmed back-bencher and the back-bencher-on-the-make looking to committees for advancement and authority rather than depending upon the party leadership. Every committee would be a power-base subversive to the party system and to government authority.

What powers would a secret services supervisory committee (were it to be established) have in relation to the executive – the Prime Minister, the Foreign Secretary and the Home Secretary? Would it release reports revealing secrets? Suppose, for example, the committee inquired into the 1946–51 Albanian operation. For five years the Secret Intelligence Service attempted to run agents into Albania to organise resistance to the communist regime of Enver Hoxha. From 1948 the operation was conducted jointly with the US Central Intelligence Agency. In 1950 SIS realised that the operation was completely compromised and withdrew. The Americans continued. More than three hundred individuals lost their lives during the course of the operation. Subsequently it was discovered that the British traitor Kim Philby had kept the Soviets informed of the detailed operational planning throughout. What would the committee do about this? Would it lay the facts before Parliament and implicitly encourage a witch-hunt a generation later? Would it be complicit and not investigate the affair? Or would it seek to investigate the affair, not present a detailed report, but recommend that Parliament take certain steps without explaining why? There is no way the toing and froing that would be involved could take place in the British system of one locus of power. If you create two or more centres of power and influence in one locus, you are prescribing chaos. It would constantly be to ask government MPs if they were supporters of the government or not. It would·be to place a double duty on everyone, asking all the time if they were party loyalists or not.

Royal Commissions are the traditional British device for investigating thorny questions. They are quite different from parliamentary committees. They are composed of outsiders. They are specific. They have no executive or legislative power. They appear, lay a document before Parliament and dissolve. They have no continuing function. For proponents of a permanent secret services supervisory committee to cite the 1982–3 Franks Committee (which was tantamount to a Royal Comission) on the Falklands war as a model for the continuous supervision of the secret services is completely to ignore its specific, temporary and powerless nature. And while Franks and his colleagues (two Labour and two Conservative Privy Councillors, and one independent member, appointed by bipartisan agreement) found things to criticise in the government's handling of pre-war incidents and of the war itself, it concluded unanimously with a clean bill of health for the government: 'We conclude that we would not be justified in attaching any criticism or blame to the present Government for the Argentine Junta's decision to commit its act of unprovoked aggression in the invasion of the Falkland Islands on 2nd April 1982.' If it had concluded otherwise, the government's parliamentary majority would have been deployed to reject or second-guess it.

In great issues, the function of Parliament is to act as a whole. In the seven major wars that the United Kingdom has fought in the last two hundred years, only two Prime Ministers have survived through a war: Pitt in the American revolutionary war and Salisbury in the Boer War. Parliament is not geared to fine-tune decision-making; that is the job of the Cabinet and individual ministers. Parliament is a focus. It is not equipped to have innumerable centres of executive power within it. It is a place where groups face each other, where there is a majority and a minority. Parliament is most effective at criticising government when it removes a Prime Minister. It is unrealistic to think that it would surrender its effectiveness to any other body or group.

Decision-making and Accountability

The quality of decision-making in government generally reflects the quality of expert debate on a subject. Most experts in any particular area have never been in government, and these experts have always been expected to start and to inform national debates. We do not, for example, look to civil servants and politicians to inform us about the merits and demerits of nuclear power stations. We look to nuclear engineers both for the facts of the case and to inform the decision-makers. The more information made public on the subject, the better in turn the popular debate and the better the decisions made by inexpert civil servants and ministers, not least because they can be scrutinised and tested by a better-informed electorate.

The task, therefore, is to bring experts into debate that informs and guides decision-making. And since the world is at Britain's door, we have no reason to think that our experts are the best in any particular subject. So the question of secrecy again arises; if we are to obtain the best thinking in our interests, then we have to ensure that the cloak of secrecy is withdrawn from all but the necessary secrets of national security. This is what Japan did after the Second World War, building its manufacturing and electronics industries in an acceptance that experts in other countries knew better than people in Japan. They did not insist that their own traditional manufacturing methods, both of production and of management, were essential to their effort. Nor did they insist that their production processes were secret. They depended upon developing a qualitative and cost-effective advantage. The Japanese acted with open minds and the determined application of expert advice.

However, the British public does not ordinarily know about decision-making. When a government changes, the Civil Service routinely denies the new government its predecessor's papers. What purpose is served by this secrecy? That the records cannot be used to fuel slanging-matches between the parties? The procedure in fact acts to protect the Civil Service and help to prevent it from looking foolish as it somersaults to accommodate contradictory policies, selectively marshalling facts to justify policies and decisions made for political or ideological reasons.

The twenty-five-year rule acts to protect the Civil Service in exactly the same way as the procedure for the non-disclosure of papers of predecessors in government. The justification advanced for the rule is that a shorter period would make officials feel compromised by the prospect of the publication of their decision-making during their working lives. But there is no evidence to suggest that the secrecy that the twenty-five-year rule provides ensures better decision-making. If anything, the evidence of Britain's decline in the world suggests the opposite.

It is impossible to believe that the Civil Service is so omnicompetent that it deserves the trust it is given. In 1954 in the Crichel Down affair, which was a Civil Service blunder (some land taken for wartime purposes was not released back to its owner as promised), the only way Sir Thomas Dugdale (later Lord Crathorne), Minister of Agriculture and Fisheries, could register his view of the competence of his civil servants was to resign. In 1982 when Lord Carrington resigned as Foreign Secretary upon the outbreak of the Falklands war nobody thought he was personally responsible for the war or for Britain being surprised by the Argentinian invasion of the islands. His resignation was his comment on the performance of the Foreign Office and the Secret Intelligence Service. In 1986 Sir Robert Armstrong, attempting historical argument, became ridiculous in an effort to justify Civil Service rules of secrecy. This happened when he gave evidence for the Crown in the prosecution it brought in Australia to prevent the publication by a retired civil servant, Peter Wright, of his memoirs of his career in SIS counter-intelligence. Sir Robert was forced to admit that, although Wright was not revealing secrets in his memoirs, Civil Service rules meant that he should not be allowed to publish. It was a classic example of the Civil Service trying to protect itself from scrutiny.

The consensual nature of British political culture again comes into play. Most mistakes and bad decisions are forgiven as long as they reflect the consensus at the time they are made. But is this constructive? Does it make Britain more effective? Does it inspire confidence in officialdom? The short answer is no, it does none of these things. Quite the contrary, it enables sloppy thinking, inefficiency and – at times – corruption to flourish. In 1956 over Suez, for example, who ever paid for the mess? Sir Anthony Eden resigned, not because of a vote of no confidence by Parliament or his Cabinet, but because he was very ill. No one resigned or was dismissed for bad judgement, bad planning, bad diplomacy. Suez, in this respect, demonstrated that in Britain accountability is secondary to being within the consensus.

Accountability exists to a greater degree in the United States because, paradoxically, decision-makers are freer than in Britain. In the USA decision-makers are more usually elected than in Britain, where they are mostly unelected permanent officials. They have fixed and limited tenure, and the political system has no whips. Decision-making in the USA is all a matter of argument. Nothing is sacred in

Congress. In Britain, argument is always cut short – guillo-tined – because government cannot tolerate intense debate. If the House of Commons, upon which government depends for its majority, were to indulge in American levels of argument, what would happen to government majorities? In any intense debate, it is likely that the government view would be seen to be a minority one.

The UK government only rarely holds majority views, which is completely separate from controlling a majority in the Commons. It is likely, for example, that the 1984 debate on the siting of London's third international airport, if allowed to run its course without being guillotined, would have found majority opinion against it being sited at Stansted. There would have been stronger pressure for London not to have a third airport at all, but for northern England to secure the commercial benefits of airport and communications develop-ments. There would have been more consideration of alterna-tive sites. There would have been fundamental questioning of the assumptions and decisions that had already been made that the investment in a third London airport, and the dislocations it would cause, would be rewarded commercially and qualitatively ten to fifteen years in the future. To allow such debate would be to challenge government control of its majority, because it would probably reveal that there was no majority for any single proposal, including the one made to the House by the government.

This is the true situation governing information, debate and accountability in Britain. Government requirements and Civil Service self-protection combine to restrict them all. The Civil Service will, naturally, work to achieve its institutional and bureaucratic objectives, and its view of the best resolution of any problem (which may not be the best objective resolution). Politicians, too, seek to achieve their view of the best resolution of a problem (which, again, may not actually be the best). Politicians will also seek to avoid being seen as in the control of the Civil Service, although the vast majority of decisions made in the name of a minister are, in fact, made by civil servants and simply endorsed by ministers. Ministers are politicians and have to spend as much as half their time in Cabinet, in Cabinet committees, in the House of Commons, on constituency work or making political speeches and visits. They simply do not have time to administer or to manage.

We vest power in Parliament and curtail debate because intense argument about any specific issue would be likely to result in the government of the day failing to secure a necessary working majority. We fudge this by keeping the level of debate low, as is manifest whenever we tune into 'Yesterday in Parliament' on the radio or attend debates and Question Time in the visitors' gallery. Parliament already contains as much debate as it can. If everybody had to stand up and be counted in Parliament and in the Civil Service, as happens in the United States, it would be a nightmare. It works in the USA because there the system is different. In Britain what we must do is secure better debate *outside* Parliament, which in turn will focus and improve the limited debate that takes place within Parliament.

An Improved Flow of Information

Having more information available, however, is separate from the operating restrictions of the political system. The question of supervision of government secrecy is also separate from the question of information availability. There is no need to assume that there is enough information made available on any subject. And while full disclosure accompanied by debate would collapse the democratic system, making vastly more information about decision-making public would not. Indeed, it would be a statement of democratic self-confidence. More information could easily be channelled to inform discussion and debate outside government, Parliament and the Civil Service, and then feed back into the political system. Parliament should be forced to pick up and focus arguments rather than initiate them, and this requires information. In turn, such a development would generate the demand for information.

The question that needs to be addressed is how to raise the level of debate by increasing the flow of information. Not by having privileged committees digging into matters: that, as I have argued, is to disperse authority and encourage chaos. Nor can it be done by legislation alone, because of the way the political system operates. It can be done through a simple determination by all those interested in public affairs not to accept certain traditions in Britain, in the same way that Robin Day simply refused to accept that Cabinet shuffles were in the realm of state secrets. We need to demystify the standing of the permanent officials of alleged expertise. In Britain no legal penalty attaches to asking questions and pressing for the answers.

The job of presenting information to Parliament is the Civil Service's. But the Civil Service does not present fifty points of view on any given subject. It is not there to raise philosophical arguments. It is there to raise operational arguments. So it does not address questions of whether or not a new policy initiative should be taken. That is the job of the elected politicians. It addresses questions of how to implement policies.

The problem that this practical situation presents is also practical. Today arguments, whether philosophical or operational, inevitably extend their terms, largely because of technological advances that mean that more people are thinking about more subjects than ever before. Every individual today knows, from experience, that nothing lasts, not even parities. Exchange rates, for example, that remained static or close to static for over a century began to fluctuate fifty-five years ago. In the last generation they have lost all stability. In turn, such experience indicates the degree of connection we all have with forces, countries and policies elsewhere that we individually, and as a nation, cannot control.

The Civil Service is not geared to address such matters. For it to do so would require an enormous expansion of its capacity. And do we want it to devote itself to providing a comprehensive display on all questions? Do we want, for example, the Foreign Office to establish a group of experts that consistently argues the Soviet point of view? The Chinese? The French? Will there ever be enough people available to the Civil Service to take up all positions? Is not this best done outside the political system, in the academic, media and commercial worlds? The positions should be argued, but they can be argued well only by maximising the flow of information to all concerned and by bringing an end to much of the secrecy enveloping decision-making in Britain.

People would not be so preoccupied with secrets if Britain had a record of success. And what is involved is not technical but economic secrets and the consensual appreciation of Britain's prospects, resources and abilities. The consensus among decision-makers has been wrong time and time again, but this has never been apparent at the crucial moments because of lack of information and the concomitant lack of informed debate. The consensus has been an ignorant one. What is more, secrecy has been used to prevent retrospective scrutiny of decision-making in time to affect the quality of current decision-making. Twenty-five years is too long. Today, for example, it would be useful to know what agreements the Bank of England has with the other central banks when we debate economic policies. Are the agreements the best available? What is their effect? Do they restrict policy options or do they enhance them? Should the answers to these questions remain official secrets?

Civil Service secrecy needs to be challenged and reduced. We should intensify argument outside Parliament and Whitehall through the contemporary (and not simply the retrospective) release of information. We should have fewer secrets, not so much in the intelligence and national security area (which, in any case, is relatively minor); the fact that Britain has spy satellites does not affect most people apart from in the most general sense. Economic and financial matters are far more important to people's lives and the country's future.

Political discourse can only be improved by the state not giving itself the benefit of the doubt at every point. The core of secrecy necessary for any state to conduct its business needs to be protected, and a working commission could be established to determine what should be classified. A new Official Secrets Act should be based on its findings, the hallmark of which should be common sense. It should establish time limits for categories, some of which might be indefinite. Throughout, the rule of reason should apply.

A Freedom of Information Act in Britain would also improve matters by speeding up the release of archives and thereby enabling people to scrutinise recent decision-making and be better informed about how decisions are made and on what bases. It would dispense with the twenty-five-year rule and it need not operate in the area of national security. By dealing with the archives it would deal, by definition, with what was no longer current. It would not operate to make public the papers in officials' desks and briefcases, or working papers generally. But it would have a knock-on effect, keeping those involved in decision-making on their toes, forcing them to be seen to take account of expert advice. Seeing the unfinished product within the decision-making process – the working papers and drafts – is far more instructive than seeing the final decision. It would make officials and ministers far more accountable. It would not achieve perfection, but would shorten time-spans and reduce secrecy, so encouraging more contemporaneous information release. The parliamentary majority would always be able to extend or restrict its application on a case-by-case basis. But it would be an improvement; it would help shake attitudes and prevent the Civil Service being the sole proprietor of the mystique of decision-making.

The release of information should not be equated with Parliamentary scrutiny. Parliamentary scrutiny is the retrospective scrutiny of intention and, to a limited degree, of final results. It is not the scrutiny of policy options and of process that Britain needs. Parliament has never engaged in the scrutiny of things while they happen and is not composed to do so. But improving the flow of information will improve the quality of questioning and hence of decision-making. It will reduce the degree to which government and the Civil Service can determine the areas and terms of debate, and it will help focus and improve accountability to Parliament. In totalitarian states, secrecy is the uniform of power; in a democracy it should be kept to a sensible minimum.

The Case for a Bill of Rights

Michael Zander

The chief reason for having a Bill of Rights is that there is no better way of strengthening the powers of the citizen against the state. The powers of the state in the modern era have become inexorably greater and more all-pervasive, and, by the same token, individuals feel themselves increasingly powerless. Democratic countries do, of course, provide a variety of mechanisms to enable citizens with a grievance to assert themselves, to take up the cudgels on their own behalf. They can write to their MP or the Ombudsman; they can attempt to get the media or like-minded citizens to mobilise with them in a campaign; they may even be able to go to law by bringing a legal action to claim their rights. But if the existing law is against them or the Ombudsman rejects their complaint or the government refuses to budge, they have no further recourse other than simply continuing their campaign in the hope that something will turn up.

A Bill of Rights is a means whereby citizens may be able to get rights that would not otherwise be available because one cannot be defeated by the state of the existing law. Even if there is a statute which seemingly authorises the grievance of which they complain, they can challenge it by bringing their action in the courts claiming that the statute is in breach of the Bill of Rights. If the claim is upheld, the Bill of Rights will take precedence. A Bill of Rights, in other words, can deal with grievances that other remedies cannot reach.

A remedy obtainable through the courts is a uniquely potent weapon. Even merely to be able to bring an action is a significant use of power. The issue of the writ means that an argument that might otherwise be ignored by government must be addressed, or else judgement will be given for the citizen. Government cannot adopt its usual posture of ignoring what it finds inconvenient or unpalatable. It must pay attention, it must produce its arguments in open court, and the arguments must be sufficiently good to persuade the court. Both sides can appeal an unfavourable ruling, and as their case goes up through the appeal process citizens have an opportunity to create additional support for their campaign. By the time that it reaches the final appeal court, even if they lose the battle, they may have won the war. The government may have successfully defended its position in the courts but at the cost of losing credibility for its position. Political realities may then dictate that the government should concede the point by changing the law. Even if the government stands firm, defending the indefensible, opposition parties may have been persuaded by the argument that a change in the law is needed, so that when in due course they form the government they may do what their predecessor refused to do. Campaigners need to take the long view. A remedy that is not available immediately may nevertheless be won over a period of time. A Bill of Rights, at the very least, is there as a way of holding government more accountable.

The European Convention on Human Rights

In one sense the argument whether the UK should have a Bill of Rights is academic; it already has one, in the form of the European Convention on Human Rights. Citizens with a grievance arguably covered by the terms of the European Convention can take it to the European Commission in Strasbourg. This possibility has now existed for twenty years since the Labour government of Harold Wilson announced in December 1965 that individuals would in future be permitted to use the right of individual petition under the Convention against the UK government. Remarkably, the decision was not thought worthy of discussion by the Cabinet or a Cabinet subcommittee. As Anthony Lester QC observed later: 'Thus was the substance, if not the form, of parliamentary sovereignty over fundamental rights transferred from London to Strasbourg not with a roar but with a whisper.'* In terms of civil liberties the importance of this event cannot be exaggerated. It is unquestionably the single most significant event of modern times in the field of protection of human rights in Britain.

The European Convention protects a variety of civil and political rights. The most important are: the right to life; the right to liberty and security of the person; the right to the fair administration of justice; respect for private and family life, home and correspondence; freedom of thought, conscience and religion; freedom of expression and to hold opinions; freedom of peaceful assembly and association, including the right to join a trade union; the right to marry and found a family. The Convention prohibits torture and inhuman or degrading treatment and punishment, slavery, servitude and forced labour; retroactive criminal laws; and discrimination in the enjoyment of rights and freedoms guaranteed by the Convention.

The machinery of the European Convention – with the Commission, the Court and the Committee of Ministers – is the most effective international mechanism for the protection of human rights yet devised. The machinery works. It delivers actual remedies in cases against governments. Under Article 53 of the Convention the High Contracting Parties undertook 'to abide by the decision of the court in any case to which they are parties', and the record of compliance has been reasonably good – though in some cases the UK government has complied reluctantly and sometimes with a good deal of foot-dragging. But, broadly, the judgements of the Court are complied with. Sometimes the remedy for the complainant comes not through a decision of the Court itself but through

*'Fundamental Rights: The United Kingdom Isolated?' *Public Law*, 1984, p. 61.

the procedure for 'friendly settlement' or through the Committee of Ministers.

Applicants first send their complaint to the Commission, which decides whether or not it is admissible. Most complaints fail at this first hurdle. The most typical ground for a finding that the complaint is inadmissible is that it has not been brought within the strict six-month time limit. Another is that complainants have not exhausted the remedies open to them in their own country. If the case is admissible, the next stage is investigation of the complaint by the Commission, which has to 'ascertain the facts' and 'to place itself at the disposal of the parties concerned with a view to securing friendly settlement of the matter'. If no settlement is reached the Commission draws up a report on the facts stating whether in its estimation they disclose a breach of the Convention. The report is sent to the Committee of Ministers of the Council of Europe.

The case can then be brought to the European Court of Human Rights by the Commission or by one of the parties. Each of the twenty-two member countries has a judge on the court. Of the first fourteen cases brought against the UK, the government lost no less than twelve.

The three alternatives of 'friendly settlement', the Committee of Ministers and the decisions of the Strasbourg Court provide a real source of strength for individuals in the member countries, whether they are citizens of those countries or not.

When the UK first ratified the European Convention in 1951, and for many years after, the Strasbourg option to petition against the UK government was hardly treated as a serious proposition. This dismissive attitude continued for some years. To read that someone had appealed to the European Commission in Strasbourg was widely treated as approximately the same as hearing of an appeal to the Queen — a sure sign of a lost cause. But during the late 1970s and the early 1980s, as the government lost case after case, this attitude gradually changed. There was the decision in 1975 in the case of Mr Sidney Golder in Parkhurst prison, whose action required a change in the prison rules regarding access to solicitors. In 1978 the government lost the case brought against it by the Irish government arising out of maltreatment by the security services of IRA suspects. In the same year judicial birching in the Isle of Man was held to be contrary to the Convention. In 1979 the Court ruled that the House of Lords decision holding that it would be contempt of court for the *Sunday Times* to publish an article accusing the Distillers Company of negligence in marketing the drug thalidomide was itself contrary to the Convention. Later cases resulted in judgement for railway workers who complained of the operation of the closed shop by British Rail, for mental patients complaining of the inadequacy of the procedure for review of their status and for a mother complaining about corporal punishment in Scottish schools.

In August 1984 in the *Malone* case the Court ruled that the UK government was in breach of the Convention in regard to its system of telephone tapping in not providing appropriate guarantees against abuses. This case was one of the most important and dramatic so far decided against the British government. Nothing could be more central to the government's apparatus of control of citizens than the power to tap their telephones secretly. The government argued that an aggrieved person had remedies against unlawful telephone tapping in both the civil and criminal courts. In the event of any interception or disclosure of intercepted material effected by a Post Office employee 'contrary to duty' or 'improperly', and without a warrant of the Secretary of State, a criminal offence would be committed under the Telegraph Acts 1863 and 1868 and the Post Office (Protection) Act 1984 (as regards telephone interceptions). On complaint that phones had been unlawfully tapped, it would be the duty of the police to investigate the matter and to initiate a prosecution if satisfied that an offence had been committed. If the police failed to prosecute, it would be open to complainants themselves to commence a private prosecution. In addition, in a case of unlawful interception by a Post Office employee without a warrant, an individual could obtain an injunction from an

English court to restrain any Post Office employee from carrying out further such interceptions or divulging the contents of such communications. Unauthorised interference with mail would also constitute the actionable wrongs of trespass to chattels. The government argued that in addition to these judicial remedies a person complaining of unlawful telephone tapping could lodge a complaint against the police, or to the Home Secretary.

In spite of all these assurances the European Court held that English law on this matter was not consistent with the Convention: 'In the opinion of the Court, the law of England and Wales does not indicate with reasonable clarity the scope and manner of exercise of the relevant discretion conferred on the public authorities. To that extent, the minimum degree of legal protection to which citizens are entitled under the rule of law in a democratic society is lacking.' As a result the English system had to be altered.* If proof were needed, this ruling showed that the European remedy has bite and that the Court could deal effectively with highly sensitive issues such as state security. Any tendency to regard the European Convention on Human Rights as inconsequential or a platform simply for 'nuts' or 'cranks' has long since disappeared. It is recognised as a serious institution capable of grappling with major problems.

Why UK Legislation Is Needed

Why, then, should there be so much dispute as to whether Britain should have a Bill of Rights? If one actually exists in Strasbourg, what is the argument about? The answer is that a

---

*See the Investigation of Communications Act 1985, though it is arguable that the new provisions do not comply with the spirit of the Strasbourg Court's ruling.

Bill of Rights in the UK, though theoretically the same, would in practice be somewhat different. The difference would lie in three main areas. First, at the most obvious pragmatic level a remedy available through the local courts should normally be quicker. The Strasbourg remedy takes an astonishingly long time to obtain. The *Golder* case, the *Sunday Times* case and the *Malone* case each took five years. Five or six years is the norm. English court procedures are slow, but not that slow. Also, in England, full legal aid is obtainable by those whose means qualify them for such help. There is no equivalently developed system of legal aid in Strasbourg. But the most important reason for having a UK Bill of Rights as opposed to one available only in Strasbourg is that it would in practice almost certainly be used far more because it would be felt to be more accessible psychologically.

A UK Bill could be utilised in any case in any civil or criminal court, from the magistrate's court to the House of Lords. Its availability would be better known to the general practitioner. At present, most barristers and solicitors have never had occasion to utilise the European Convention. Even assuming they know anything about the Convention, they are unfamiliar with its terms and its interpretation by the Commission and the Court and with its procedure. Knowing little or nothing about it naturally reinforces the tendency not to use the machinery. By contrast, if it became a remedy available in the English courts they would have heard about it and would quickly learn how to use it. Articles in the legal press about the process of utilising the Bill of Rights would be felt by practitioners to be relevant to their ordinary work for their clients – instead of as now being regarded as of interest only to a few Strasbourg specialists. For anyone who believes that a Bill of Rights would be a beneficial innovation, its availability in the UK courts would therefore be a positive advantage. Conversely, anyone who fears the concept would tend to prefer that it be confined to the relatively restricted role it plays in Strasbourg rather than allowing it the greater opportunity of playing on the domestic stage.

The European Convention is a treaty by which the UK is

bound internationally but, since no statute has been passed to make it part of the law of the UK, it cannot be made the subject of rights and duties in the courts of this country. In order for it to be available for use in the UK courts it must be incorporated into UK law by statute – as was done for the EEC treaties by the European Communities Act 1972. The argument about the desirability of a Bill of Rights for the UK is normally put in terms of whether the European Convention should be incorporated by a statute into UK law. In theory there are other options. A free-standing, specially drafted Bill of Rights might from some points of view be preferable. The European Convention was, after all, drafted nearly forty years ago. Much has happened in the interim, and the cases brought to the Commission and the Court have naturally revealed shortcomings in the drafting and gaps that might usefully be filled. But such reflections, though valid as far as they go, are unrealistic. There is little enough prospect that any Bill of Rights would be acceptable to a British government of the foreseeable future. There is no prospect that any government would contemplate drafting a Bill of Rights in different terms from those of the Convention. The Convention has now been in force for several decades. British governments of both the Labour Party and the Conservative Party have operated it. They are familiar with the process and the text. They have accepted its jurisdiction and have implemented rulings of the Court based on its present scope. It may not be perfect in all respects but it is not so imperfect as to have required either party to commit itself to withdrawal or to repeal of the present text. This negative approval is significant. The fact that both main parties have been content to operate in government under the present text (and periodically to renew the right of individual petition, as both have done) is clear indication that, whatever its defects, the Convention as it stands can be made to work and has no insuperable problems. Certainly, all participants in the debate have argued from the perspective of incorporation of the European Convention as the only practical approach. The House of Lords Select Committee in its report in 1978 was divided 6–5 in favour of a Bill of Rights but was unanimous 11–0 that if there was to be a Bill of Rights it would have to be the European Convention.*

One obvious advantage of incorporation from the British government's point of view is that many cases that now reach Strasbourg would be dealt with internally. The embarrassment of being constantly 'in the dock' in Strasbourg would be reduced. In fact the number of cases brought against the UK is consistently one of the highest brought against any of the member states per head of the population. There are various possible explanations of this phenomenon. One is that civil liberties are more frequently abused in Britain than in other European countries. This does not seem likely. A more probable explanation is that Britain has the largest number of experienced and sophisticated civil liberties lawyers and civil liberties organisations, such as the National Council for Civil Liberties and MIND (which protects the interests of the mentally ill and mentally handicapped). But a third possible explanation is that Britain is the only country in Europe which does not have a Bill of Rights.

It is true that cases which were brought in the UK courts could still end up in Strasbourg by way of appeal. But this is so only of cases in which the complainant is the loser in the UK. If the complainant won in the UK courts, the case could not be brought to Strasbourg by the government. A government can be the complainant only in an action against another state, as in the case brought against the UK by the Irish state over the maltreatment of IRA terrorist suspects. So this is a further respect in which a Bill of Rights favours citizens against the state and strengthens their position. Even if they lose in their own courts, they still have the opportunity to try again in Strasbourg.

*Report of the Select Committee on a Bill of Rights, House of Lords, paper 176, June 1978.

The Protection of Civil Liberties

Another advantage of having a Bill of Rights is that it strengthens not merely the citizen with a grievance but the whole apparatus of protection of civil liberties. Britain, by comparison with most, is a country where civil liberties are tolerably well protected. When the UK ratified the European Convention, the government was advised that it was perfectly safe to ratify since it was unlikely that there would be many instances of cases brought successfully against it. This prediction has proved dramatically wrong. In fact civil liberties are not as well protected as they should be. MPs' questions to the minister are a notoriously feeble device. The Ombudsman's role is limited to maladministration. Actions in the courts can be brought successfully only if there is no binding precedent, statute or statutory instrument in the way and then only if the courts are prepared to develop a remedy from existing precedents. The protection of civil liberties is not an activity that engages the energies of mainstream British lawyers to any great extent. It is seen rather as a concern of radical lawyers in organisations like the NCCL, the Legal Action Group and the Haldane Society. If there were a Bill of Rights, civil liberties would be likely to become more of a mainstream concern of lawyers and indeed of parliamentarians, the press and anyone who takes an interest in public affairs.

Needless to say, the mere fact of having a Bill of Rights does not *guarantee* better protection of civil rights. There have been plenty of examples of countries with Bills of Rights where civil liberties were cynically abused. (Amin's Uganda had a splendid Bill of Rights.) But in a genuinely democratic country such as the UK the probability is that support for and protection of civil liberties would be strengthened rather than weakened by the introduction of a Bill of Rights, if only because it would act as a major educative force.

Moreover, a Bill of Rights is an instrument capable of responding to problems as they arise. An ordinary statute is closed in the sense that it can deal only with the matters that are covered by its terms. Even given the most liberal canons of construction there are severe limits to what can be said to be within the meaning of the statute. A Bill of Rights by contrast is open ended. The broad and somewhat vague phrases of a Bill of Rights have much more capacity to expand to meet changing circumstances than the words of a normal statute. Some take this to be a disadvantage of a Bill of Rights, since it makes things unpredictable. The words mean what the judges say they mean. (The pros and cons of the judicial role are considered below.) But the advantage is that the citizen with a grievance may be able to seek a remedy whether or not it is something on which the legislature has passed a law. Unless Parliament has specifically dealt with the precise matter in derogation of the Bill of Rights, the courts will be free to interpret the Bill of Rights so as to deal with problems as they arise. A Bill of Rights, in other words, is a flexible and adaptable tool to deal with civil liberties concerns as they present themselves from time to time.

A Bill of Rights also has the advantage that it places the power of action in the hands of the person who claims to be aggrieved. If the relief of grievances is left to governments and the executive, too often it will be more convenient to do nothing. If individuals can raise their complaints before an impartial tribunal where they can be heard, where they can publicly contest the arguments put by or on behalf of officials and from which they can get an actual decision, the system to that extent becomes more responsive and more politically sensitive.

The burden of proof will usually be on the state rather than on the citizen. The technical position as to who has the burden of proof often determines the outcome of litigation. Under the Bill of Rights, once an infringement of rights has been established, it is for the defendant to justify the infringement. So under the European Convention the citizen is given the right to liberty and security of person, the right to a fair and public hearing, the right to respect for private and family life, home and correspondence, etc. But each of these rights is said to be qualified. Thus the right to respect for privacy under Article 8 is said to be subject to the qualification that any infringement is permitted only if it is in accordance with law and 'is necessary in a democratic society in the interests of national security, public safety or the economic well-being of the country, for the prevention of disorder or crime, for the protection of health or morals, or for the protection of the rights and freedom of others'.

At first sight, this may look like nonsense on stilts. The citizen is given a comprehensive right which is then comprehensively emasculated by the qualifying clauses. Is there any point or advantage? The answer, decidedly, is yes. Unless the state can justify the invasion of his or her rights, the citizen wins. The burden of showing that the infringement of liberty is 'necessary' is not easy to discharge. In the *Golder* case, for example, the citizen won because the state could not establish that the rules limiting the access of prisoners to solicitors were 'necessary' in a democratic society to prevent disorder or crime. The Home Office may have had reasons for thinking that these rules were desirable or conducive to good order in the prisons but it could not show that they were necessary. So the government lost. Many of the other cases lost by the UK government have been crucially affected in the same way by the burden of proof factor.

The United States Bill of Rights does not have these qualifying clauses. It simply guarantees the rights covered, baldly and without apparent restriction. So US citizens have the right to freedom of expression and freedom from discrimination and a right to due process. But in reality the US courts have implied the same kind of qualifications as are explicitly recognised in the European Convention. The effect therefore is comparable. The US judge, when considering an alleged infringement of one of the basic rights, has to take account of the pros and cons of the question, as the judge in Strasbourg must do when interpreting the Convention. It is not enough for the judge to hold that there has been an infringement of one of the liberties guaranteed by the Bill of Rights. He or she must go on to determine whether the infringement is legitimate, which then brings in all the policy questions that are directly addressed in the European Convention. Such policy debates are an inevitable feature of cases on a Bill of Rights.

The Judicial Role

Can judges be expected to deal competently with policy questions involving social, economic, political and even philosophical matters? This issue has two separate elements. One is whether policy questions *can* be handled adequately in a court of law. The second is whether they *should* be handled in a court.

Obviously there are some kinds of policy questions that a court could not cope with. One would not ask a court whether the steel industry should be nationalised or whether a new hospital is needed in a new area. These are issues that are not justiciable in a court of law. But policy questions are latent in a high proportion of the cases that come to court for decision on points of law.

Even today when statutes pour thick and fast from Parliament there is still a major creative function for the judges. The importance of this role is concealed by the judicial tendency to proclaim that what the judge is doing is no more than to state what the law is. The judge does not admit that it includes an element of saying what it ought to be. Barristers inexperienced or unwise enough to address a court on what the law ought to be will find themselves out on their ear. They will be sharply reminded that a court of law is not a place for discussion of what the law ought to be. But this obscures what really happens when there is a conflict as to what the law is. Unless the court finds itself constrained by the unambiguous words of the statute or by binding precedent, it will always have a choice as to the outcome. Cases that are litigated on points of law are almost invariably ones where the lawyers for both sides have advised that there are tolerable prospects of success. It may be necessary to take an appeal as high as the House of Lords, which is not bound by any precedent and therefore always has a choice. But it is surprising how often courts are able to make up their mind rather than being confined by the strait-jacket of a binding precedent. In any such case the court is in truth deciding on policy matters and deciding what the law ought to be – even though it is always dressed up as a decision as to what the law is. Deciding legal cases is not like mathematics. There are no right and wrong answers as in mathematics. Judicial decision-making on points of law is much more a question of deciding what rule makes most sense both in the light of the previous indications in earlier precedents and any information the court may have as to the advantages and disadvantages in terms of the propositions of law advanced by the respective parties.

There is no doubt that a court room is not the ideal place to hammer out major issues of policy. The argument is confined to the two litigants, whose means and capacities may be severely limited. This is not true of the government, which has unlimited resources for the purpose of defending litigation. But private litigants may not have the money to prepare, present or pursue the case properly. The US procedure permits organisations and others who are not themselves directly engaged in the litigation to participate through written briefs which are submitted by 'friends of the court' (*amicus curiae*). So specialist interest groups can bring their expertise to bear on the problem and can contribute valuable and sometimes essential elements to the case presented by one or other party. (The NAACP, for instance, played a crucial role in civil rights cases in the US courts in the 1960s and 1970s, deploying its great experience, knowledge and skills in litigation designed to secure rights for blacks. The American Civil Liberties Union likewise frequently files a brief in cases brought under the Bill of Rights.) There is, however, no equivalent procedure in the UK. The UK court would therefore not have the views of such expert bodies available to it; it is limited to whatever material is presented by the parties.

Also, under the UK procedure there is little opportunity to present the court with relevant material which goes beyond the narrow legal sources. The courts will receive statutes and judicial precedents. These are the familiar 'stuff' from which English judges fashion their judgements. But the court will be far less ready to entertain economic, social and other relevant data drawn from non-legal sources. The tradition of UK courts is to consider legal issues on the basis of legal source materials in a narrow sense. The European Court of Human Rights, by contrast, receives a broader range of argumentation. Maybe this broader approach would spill over to the UK courts if the Convention were to be available for use. But this is not certain.

But even if it is admitted that policy issues *can* be addressed in UK courts it does not follow that they *should* be. One's approach to this problem turns basically on a general view of the respective roles of courts and legislatures. In most democratic countries it is assumed that law-making is the task of the legislature, while the role of the courts is to interpret the will of Parliament and in a common-law country to develop the law through precedent. According to this model, Parliament makes the law, whilst the judges interpret, develop, find or discover the law. But this is in reality too simple an account of how the system works. In fact the judges have always played a creative role both in interpreting statutes and even more in adapting the common law to changing circumstances. Great areas of the law were created by the judges with little or no intervention by Parliament, especially in former times.

It is desirable that if the courts are to deal with policy issues they should be as fully informed as possible of relevant facts and other considerations that bear on the decision. Naturally, in a court of law the arguments will always be canvassed on a narrower basis than in a legislature; but there is no good reason for arbitrarily and unnecessarily limiting the nature of arguments that can be deployed in the course of litigation. The sole question should be whether the matters referred to are relevant to the legal issue before the court. On the first question therefore the answer is that policy issues can certainly be addressed in a court but that UK procedure would need some reform if this was to be done as effectively as possible.

Policy issues are therefore, and always have been, part of judicial decision-making on points of law. But it is still legitimate to argue that the consequence of a Bill of Rights is to give an unwelcome boost to the extent of such judicial policy-making. This was the burden of Lord McCluskey's recent Reith Lectures in which he strongly argued against the incorporation of the European Convention on the ground that it would involve the judges in many issues which ought rather to be the preserve of the legislature: 'The cobbler should stick to his last. The judge should be confined to resolve disputes by applying the law. Law-making should be left to law-makers, policy-making to responsible policy-makers.'* Lord McCluskey appeared even to deny that judges do in fact decide important policy issues. His view would be widely shared amongst British judges, who fear being exposed to the criticism that they are doing the legislature's work. Such activities are often couched in terms of abuse – 'Who do these unelected judges think they are, deciding matters of public controversy? Not only are they unaccountable but they are drawn from a narrow social class, and their professional lives have been lived in the cloistered backwater of the Inns of Court, amongst other lawyers and judges.'

There is no denying that judges do on the whole come from a narrow social class. Every survey ever done shows the English bench to be predominantly drawn from people (mostly male) who have been to public schools and Oxbridge. Their professional formation is also relatively narrow in that most of them spend their lives in and around the courts. On the other hand, they see something of the real world through the prism of the problems brought to them by their lay clients. A barrister whose professional life has been spent prosecuting and defending in criminal cases, for instance, probably knows more than he or she cares to about the seamier side of life.

---

*'Trusting the Judges', *The Listener*, 27 November 1986, p. 13.

Barristers whose work has included family law and personal injury work have likewise seen a good deal of how the 'real world' lives.

Although a court room may not be the ideal place to determine a matter of policy, it may not be a bad place to decide a question of principle. The history of the legislative attitude to the blacks in the United States in the first six decades of the twentieth century does not inspire confidence in the capacity of legislators to do the morally right thing when the instinct of the voters is to maintain an immoral status quo. It was judges, not the legislature, that gave meaning to the ideal of equality in the US constitution. Similarly, the rights of prisoners in the USA have been protected in the past twenty years not by legislatures but by courts using the Bill of Rights provisions concerning cruel and unusual punishment. There are few votes in the protection of ill-favoured minorities such as blacks and prisoners. But the protection of minorities from the tyranny of the majority is the authentic business of civil liberties, and sometimes judges who do not face an election may be more responsive to the call of moral principles than the politicians whose stock-in-trade is fudge and mudge.

According to one school of thought, this is unlikely to be true of English judges, whose basic instincts, it is argued, are to support the establishment, the status quo, the conservative position. For those who share this view, to have a Bill of Rights would be to make a bad situation worse – out of the frying-pan into the fire. Professor John Griffith, the guru for this faction, especially in his provocative book *The Politics of the Judiciary*, has suggested that the English judicial attitude to the public interest is shown by 'tenderness towards private property and dislike of trade unions, strong adherence to the maintenance of order, distaste for minority opinions, demonstrations and protests, indifference to the promotion of better race relations, support of government secrecy, concern for the preservation of the moral and social behaviour to which it is accustomed'.*

*Fontana, 2nd ed., 1981, p. 237.

Griffith's analysis, however, leaves too much out of account. There are indeed many examples that what he says is the dominant posture of the English judges, but there are also many counter-examples which illustrate the opposite tendency. Every self-respecting trade unionist would subscribe to the Griffith view that the courts are generally against the trade unions. Yet a study of all the reported judicial decisions in this area from 1871 to 1966 showed that, whilst 79 were decided against the interests of the workers, no less than 48 went the other way. If the Griffith thesis were correct, one might have expected that the balance of decisions would have been ten or at least five to one.* A ratio of six to three hardly demonstrates that the judges are invincibly biased against trade unionists. Similarly with many other fields: there are plenty of decisions which show the judges willing and able to protect the citizen against the state, as well as many other decisions which show the judges supporting the state. The record is mixed.

It may not be the case that one can confidently trust the judges. But equally one cannot confidently trust the legislature. It is wiser to assume that no human institution can be trusted to do the right thing consistently. If this is correct, the best course is to arrange things so that both have their respective chance to correct injustice and to remedy grievances. The legislature is the main author of new law and should always have the last word. Even if there were a Bill of Rights it could not prevent Parliament from repealing or amending it. In a democracy the majority can in the end have its way. That is the price one pays for the democratic system. Even a requirement of a two-thirds or three-quarters majority is no protection if Parliament is virtually unanimous, as it was in passing the Official Secrets Act in 1911 and the Prevention of Terrorism (Temporary Provisions) Act 1974 in the wake of the Birmingham bombing by the IRA. But a requirement of a two-thirds or three-quarters majority is anyway probably unenforceable in the British constitution. The judges would

---

*Paul O'Higgins and Martin Partington, 'Industrial Conflict: Judicial Attitudes', *Modern Law Review*, 32, 1969, p. 53.

not recognise it. The highest form of entrenchment likely to work in the British constitution is a rule that any amendment or repeal of the Bill of Rights must be explicit to take effect. This would still leave ultimate power where it belongs in a democracy: with the legislature. But the legislature would naturally be slow to be seen to be meddling with the Bill of Rights. So, in practice, amendments would be rare, and there would be a significant measure of entrenchment *de facto* even if not *de jure*.

If the United States experience is any guide, most cases brought under a Bill of Rights do not involve dramatic clashes between the court and the legislature. They concern rather low-level disputes where a citizen has arguably had his or her rights infringed by a police officer, immigration officer, local politician or bureaucrat. Occasionally the US courts have been asked to hold a statute unconstitutional. But for every one such case there have been a hundred or more raising issues of much less dramatic import. Students protesting against the Vietnam War are prevented from wearing armbands in school; a citizen says that his right to have a collection of pornography at home is protected by the constitution; a ban on a march by neo-Nazis in a public park is challenged as an infringement of the right of free speech; conditions in the prison system of a state are held to be unconstitutional.* Questions of that order are much more common than conflicts between the courts and the legislature. These are disputes on which the view of a judge is not inappropriate. In fact a judge is probably better able to deal with such questions than the legislature.

The argument over a Bill of Rights turns ultimately on whether one trusts the judges to make a reasonable job of it. Incorporation of the European Convention into UK law would give them a bigger and more challenging role than they have ever had before. They would be called to answer new

---

*For further examples see Michael Zander, *A Bill of Rights?*, Sweet & Maxwell, 1985, Appendix 2, p. 102.

questions which would give them a broader and more important function. This is the unavoidable consequence of giving the citizen a new way of seeking the redress of grievances. It is the judge who must adjudicate on whether the grievance deserves a remedy. Britain is almost the only democratic country in the world that does not have a Bill of Rights. It would seem remarkable if the British judges were not fit for a task that judges throughout the world perform, the protection of the citizen against the state, a task the judges claim to perform. A Bill of Rights in essence is a means for them to perform that task more effectively and more often.

Against a Bill of Rights?

Simon Lee

Should the United Kingdom enact a Bill of Rights? This is a question of perennial fascination for lawyers and other students of the British constitution. It is given extra piquancy in 1987 since this year has seen a Private Member's Bill attempt to incorporate the European Convention on Human Rights and because the USA is this year celebrating the bicentenary of its constitution, which has, as the jewel in its crown, a Bill of Rights and a Supreme Court. Since 1987 or 1988 will be an election year in which the Alliance will include a Bill of Rights in its manifesto, and since 1988 or 1989, depending on one's accounting methods, will be the tercentenary of our own limited Bill of Rights, this tired topic deserves serious re-examination.

I propose to say nothing at all about the advantages of such a development. Professor Zander needs no encouragement in that direction. Nor do I intend to provide a comprehensive list of the arguments against a Bill of Rights. I shall not dwell, for example, on the surprising fact that the European Convention is particularly weak on the very issue which most concerns civil libertarians, namely discrimination. There is no general prohibition on discrimination. The relevant Article 14 merely bans discrimination in the exercise of the other rights and freedoms set out in the rest of the Convention. Since there is no right to work in the European Convention, the projected Bill of Rights would not even prohibit discrimination in employment. We would still have to rely on our existing British statutes and that different European network of law, the European Economic Community, for challenges to discriminatory practices. But my argument does not depend on wishing for a *better* Bill of Rights. So I shall mention only in passing that the Convention does not cover many other vital rights for our times, namely social and economic rights such as the rights some would claim we have to food, shelter and employment. Nevertheless, I do think it is important that those who argue in favour of a Bill of Rights take pains to ensure that they know exactly which rights are, and which are not, in the only plausible candidate for adoption, the European Convention on Human Rights and Fundamental Freedoms.

The question whether we should incorporate that Convention is not answered by compiling tables of pros and cons. It is a question of attitude, style and emphasis, of political, legal and constitutional culture. One has to grasp the kind of society we would become with the Bill of Rights and see how that compares with the kind of society we are and the kind we would like to be. I shall therefore first consider the need for constitutional reform in the UK and then focus on another country altogether, drawing on the experience of the United States since the US constitution is most often invoked as the paradigm for those who champion a Bill of Rights. Then I shall try to give the flavour of the European Convention as it presently operates, before considering how that would translate to the domestic British context. Finally, I will draw attention to alternative solutions to the perceived problem which the Bill of Rights seeks to address and I will cast some doubt on any preoccupation with law as the primary means of effecting change in society. We have to begin, then, by understanding what a constitution is and what the problem with our constitution is said to be.

The British Constitution and the Need for Reform

There seems to be an initial difficulty in so far as it is sometimes said that the UK does not have a constitution at all. But it does. For the word 'constitution' is used in at least two senses, only one of which is to describe that which we lack, namely a single document which sets out the rules of political authority in a state. In that sense, we do not have a constitution. But 'constitution' can also be used more broadly to refer to those fundamental rules and principles, whatever the form in which they are found. In this latter sense, we do have a constitution. Indeed, under this definition, every state must have one.

The next common fallacy is the claim that our constitution is unwritten. Again, this is nonsense. Statutes like the Parliament Acts of 1911 and 1949, which are central to our constitution, are written. Cases like the GCHQ decision are written. Even conventions like the ones about ministerial responsibility can be found on the printed page, as described by Bagehot, Dicey and contemporary commentators.

But it would also be wrong to overemphasise the formalities of our constitution. Our constitution is, admittedly, made up in large part by laws. From the Parliament Acts, which delimit the powers of our legislature, to the Race and Sex Discrimination Acts, which help safeguard civil liberties, statutes help to determine the scope of political authority in the UK. But laws alone do not tell the whole story. One example concerns the difference between the legal theory and the political reality of the Royal Assent. The legal position is that a Bill cannot become an Act of Parliament without the Royal Assent. But the more important information is that there is a convention that the sovereign will never refuse such assent. If we just learnt about the law without knowing that the last refusal was by Queen Anne in 1707, then we would misunderstand the constitutional realities.

So what are conventions? All constitutions involve conventions, but some constitutions involve more conventions that others, and the UK probably heads the list. Conventions are rules of political practice, and, in contrast to laws, there seems to be no agreement about how or when they arise or change. The word 'convention' is used to describe or criticise a multitude of practices. It is an umbrella term for customs, practices, maxims, precepts, understandings, habits or usages.

The use of the generic word conceals differences in the firmness with which the rules hold. All conventions are breakable and changeable, but some conventions are more breakable and more easily changeable than others.

Contrary to ill-informed rumour, therefore, we already have a constitution. Its fundamental principle is parliamentary sovereignty, the doctrine that Parliament can make any law whatsoever and that no court can challenge such law. This is an astonishing concept, since virtually every other state in the world imposes formal limits on the competence of its legislature. We trust instead that conventions and other practical restraints will ameliorate the inherent dangers of Parliament's absolute power.

So far I have been talking the language of constitutional lawyers. In plain English, what is our constitution all about? It could be summarised as 'a good chaps theory of government'. We can rely on the politicians to be good chaps. We don't need formal restraints. MPs have consciences and they want to get re-elected. Those are two incentives to good behaviour and two safeguards against abuse of their theoretically unlimited power. It's just not cricket to break the conventions.

But even cricket isn't cricket any more. Intimidatory bowling has led the cricket authorities to countenance helmets and other protective gear. There are new pressures on cricketers, particularly now that they are playing for high financial stakes. Times change, and so the constitution of cricket has changed. The question is whether there have been similar changes in politics and whether we should change our national constitution accordingly.

The key motivation for constitutional reform was well summarised by Lord Hailsham, the present Lord Chancellor. He once detected a worrying trend in the British constitution. The theory is, as we have seen, that Parliament (composed of the Commons, Lords and monarch) is sovereign. But in practice the Queen plays no part in legislation, the House of Lords is more or less powerless in the face of a determined Commons, the opposition parties in the Commons are powerless in the face of a determined majority party, the back-benchers in the majority are powerless in the face of the government which controls their future rise in the hierarchy, the junior ministers are powerless in the face of the Cabinet, and some would add that the Cabinet is perhaps powerless in the face of the Prime Minister. Hence parliamentary sovereignty can lead in effect to a small group of politicians, albeit elected leaders, having the opportunity to make any law they please. Lord Hailsham dubbed this the 'elective dictatorship'. He was in opposition at the time and he seems less vocal in his criticisms now that he is himself again part of that 'elective dictatorship'; but, to his credit as a man of integrity, he retains his enthusiasm for seeking solutions to the perceived problem.

Most proposals for constitutional reform are a response to that criticism. Thus, electoral reform would be designed to stop powerful governments at source. Unless they achieved the improbable feat of an overall majority of votes cast, under a system of proportional representation governments would have to compromise to achieve any power at all. Coalition governments would become the norm, and so no single political grouping could dictate; they would have to negotiate. Again, a reformed second chamber might be advocated as a more effective check on the Commons. Devolution would take some power away from the central government. Freedom of information would allow the media and citizens greater control; information equals power. And a Bill of Rights would in practice involve a transfer of power from the government, through its control of Parliament, to the judges who would interpret the Bill. Concerning that last option, there are good arguments in favour of such a move, which Professor Zander has written about, but there are also many genuine worries which cast doubt on the wisdom of such a dramatic 'solution' to the supposed problem.

Political Parties' Views

Some of those on the extreme political right and extreme left and all of those in the extreme middle can be counted among the supporters of the Bill of Rights idea. But the official stance of the Conservative and Labour parties does not embrace the reform, whereas the Alliance parties are enthusiastic supporters of such a change. Why? The historical reasons why people and parties come to hold particular views are analytically distinct from the merits of the views themselves. One can point to cynical reasons for the Alliance's adoption of all manner of reform, but that does not in itself invalidate the proposals. So what are the cynical and the noble explanations for the left, right and middle positions? ('Left', 'right' and 'middle' are often remarkably unhelpful terms, but I use them since they are common currency.)

The right endorses the 'good chaps/cricket' approach to the constitution. It wants, as the name of its party suggests, to conserve the status quo. It is suspicious of change. There is good reason for such caution in constitutional matters, because the constitution affects everything else. But this is not conclusive. The constitution is perpetually in flux, as demonstrated by the dramatic and constant development of the franchise over the last two centuries. In a nutshell, the right trusts in the traditional picture of self-restraint which has already been outlined.

The left regards politics as about power, a struggle between rival claims. Under the present political process, it can aspire to complete power half the time. Under a Bill of Rights judges would have the effective power all the time. This would be a good move, therefore, only if Labour trusted the judges to reflect socialist ideas. But the reality is different. Labour is deeply suspicious of the judges, coming as they do from a narrow, élitist background. One might object to the relevance of that by observing that many a Labour supporter or even politician comes from a similar background without having the same views. Because judges tend to be old, white, male, rich, upper middle class, public-school and Oxbridge educated, the left tends to regard them as irredeemably right-wing. Yet Labour's Tony Benn, among others, is old, white, male, rich, upper middle class, public-school and Oxbridge educated, without being noticeably reactionary. The explanation for the difference might be that Tony Benn has not shared the judges' legal training and experience but has had a wider exposure to British society. Judges might dispute that, but for our purposes it is sufficient to record how the left feels about the judges. In particular, Labour fears that a hostile judiciary might be able to use a Bill of Rights to strike down a socialist programme.

Neither Conservatives nor Labour place constitutional change at the top of the political agenda. The voters and politicians are much more interested in the pound in their pocket, in unemployment, inflation, crime, housing and the like. Between them, the two major parties encompass most of the plausible positions on the economy. There is no space on the continuum for a distinct middle package. The old Liberal Party and especially the new SDP have therefore been pushed towards focusing on constitutional reform as a method of brand differentiation. If the cereal market comprises only Shredded Wheat and Cornflakes, someone will produce Weetabix and Frosties (Frosties being the same old recipe as Cornflakes but with a little bit of sugar on top to disguise the fact). Hence the SDP was ripe for capture by those who had some sugar, something different, to offer. Lawyers of a liberal/left disposition found that their time, or their party, had come. The 'gang of one hundred' included many lawyers like Professor Zander and Anthony Lester QC, arch-supporters of the Bill of Rights idea. Moreover, because the Alliance has had only very limited prospects of power, constraints on those who do have power would at least help protect its vision of the common good.

The current leader of the SDP, David Owen, wrote a kind of manifesto for the projected party when he left the Labour Party. In that book, *Face the Future*, he was sanguine about what leads to constitutional change. In discussing electoral reform, he took the cynical, many would say realistic, view that 'When the arguments and the mass of books and pamphlets on the subject have all been weighed, the question of electoral reform will be resolved by the pressure of power politics, not by merit or by constitutional theory about coalitions or the two-party system.'*

Dr Owen presumably felt the same way about the moves for a Bill of Rights, but we cannot be sure since there is no mention of a Bill of Rights in the entire book. Similarly, another founding text of the new party, *Politics Is for People* by Shirley Williams, does not concentrate on constitutional reform, mentioning neither a Bill of Rights nor electoral reform.† In his latest book, *A United Kingdom?*, David Owen adopts a cautious approach to some constitutional changes, such as introducing more frequent referendums; he says that it is far better to evolve than to embrace major constitutional change in a hurry.‡

Nevertheless, the Alliance has given impetus to the drive for a Bill of Rights. The momentum was already there, mostly provided by Lord Scarman's seminal Hamlyn Lectures of 1974. But what does a Bill of Rights look like and what does it do?

Bills of Rights are vague documents. Even tightly drafted laws are susceptible to different interpretations. Bills of Rights contain such broad statements as 'Everyone has the right to respect for his private and family life' (Article 8 of the European Convention), which can be applied by judges in diametrically opposed ways. Bills of Rights do not answer all the questions about our civil liberties. Those who interpret the documents have great discretion and therefore power. This was well put by Lord McCluskey in his 1986 Reith Lectures, which provided influential support for the view that we should not enact a new Bill of Rights:

---

*Face the Future, OUP, 1981, p. 180.
†Politics Is for People, Penguin, 1981.
‡A United Kingdom?, Penguin, 1986.

> The law does not have the quality of a railway timetable with predetermined answers to all the questions that human life, man's wickedness and the intricacies of commerce can throw up. . . . The law, as laid down in a code, or in a statute or in a thousand eloquently reasoned opinions, is no more capable of providing all the answers than a piano is capable of providing music. The piano needs the pianist, and any two pianists, even with the same score, may produce very different music.

So the question, as Humpty Dumpty might have said, is which is to be master — that's all. Are we going to give judges or politicians the last word in defining and developing our rights? Superficially, there is some attraction in asking the judges to adopt a greater role, as they have in more or less every other constitution in the world. But, as Lord McCluskey observed, one ought to consider why those countries needed a Bill of Rights. We might be ahead of, not behind, the field. Many Bills of Rights have been introduced as an inadequate recognition of deep problems such as discrimination by new settlers against the original inhabitants of a country. Even countries which have recently thought about adopting a Bill of Rights are not exact analogies. Canada, for example, is a federal country in which a Bill of Rights can help protect the different spheres of influence of the component parts. New Zealand, currently considering a Bill of Rights, does not have a second legislative chamber to check its lower House.

With these warnings in mind, let us look at how a Bill of Rights works in another culture, that of the United States. I choose this example since it is widely regarded as the best show-place for a Bill of Rights. By interpreting and applying the US Bill of Rights, the Supreme Court has made some notable strides forward in the establishment, protection and promotion of rights. Perhaps the US example is therefore the best setting in which to understand how a society might resolve contentious issues of civil liberties when it has a Bill of Rights.

The US Experience

Although the US Supreme Court is most often held up as the model for judges acting as interpreters of a Bill of Rights, Lord McCluskey has some doubts in his Reith Lectures:

> Even the broad, unqualified statements of rights which the Supreme Court Justices have had to apply did not prevent them, until recently, from taking a narrow, legalistic, laissez-faire perspective on freedom so as to strike down as unconstitutional legislation designed to stop the exploitation of workers, women, children or immigrants. They legalised slavery; and when it was abolished, they legalised racial segregation. They repeatedly held that women were not entitled to equality with men. They approved the unconstitutional removal by the Executive of the constitutional rights of Americans of Japanese origin after the bombing of Pearl Harbor.

Supporters and doubters both agree that the US Supreme Court has enormous power. The court's development of a doctrine of privacy without the right even appearing in the text of the US Bill of Rights is a testimony to that. The path from *Griswold* v. *Connecticut*, the 1965 case which protected a married couple's right to use contraceptives in the privacy of their bedroom, to *Roe* v. *Wade*, the 1973 case which protected a woman's decision to abort, has seemed an attractive one to many American liberals. But others have been incensed by the idea that the court has created such a right to privacy out of thin constitutional air. So the important issue is whether one can approve of the Supreme Court's power independently of liking the latest development.

Those who praised the Supreme Court in *Roe* v. *Wade*, for example, may be changing their minds after the recent 1986 decision in *Bowers, Attorney-General of Georgia* v. *Hardwick*. In that case, the constitutionality of a Georgia statute which made sodomy a criminal offence was challenged under the right to privacy. The Supreme Court upheld the constitutionality of the statute by a 5–4 majority. The majority stressed that they were not judging the wisdom or desirability of the statute but rather its constitutionality. Justice White's majority opinion examined privacy cases such as *Griswold* v. *Connecticut* and *Roe* v. *Wade* and concluded:

> We think it evident that none of the rights announced in those cases bears any resemblance to the claimed constitutional right of homosexuals to engage in acts of sodomy, that is asserted in this case. No connection between family, marriage or procreation on the one hand and homosexual activity on the other has been demonstrated.

This passage rests on two dubious points. The earlier privacy cases are depicted as being about 'family, marriage or procreation'. The instant case is regarded as being about homosexuals. Neither of these crucial assumptions is entirely convincing. *Roe* v. *Wade*, about an unmarried pregnant woman's wish for an abortion, can be described as being about family, marriage or procreation only in a negative sense. And the Georgia statute at issue in the present case did not distinguish between homosexual and heterosexual activity. The statute made it just as much a criminal offence for a married heterosexual couple to engage in oral sex as for a homosexual couple.

Justice Blackmun, the author of the majority opinion in *Roe* v. *Wade* (where Justice White and Justice Rehnquist had dissented), this time found himself in the minority. He wrote a vigorous dissent which concluded that 'depriving individuals of the right to choose for themselves how to conduct their intimate relationships poses a far greater threat to the values most deeply rooted in our nation's history than tolerance or nonconformity could ever do. Because I think the Court today betrays those values, I dissent.'

All the judgements in this case deserve an audience on this side of the Atlantic. Between them they encompass many judicial techniques and many varieties of moral judgement. The contrast between majority and minority views of the constitution is stark and revealing. It suggests that enacting a Bill of Rights does not resolve political disputes. It converts them into a legal form and forum and leaves their resolution to the chance of who happens to be on the court. This is largely a matter of luck. Firstly, a US President may have no opportunity to influence the composition of the Supreme Court, because no judge resigns, retires or dies during his tenure (Supreme Court justices have life tenure). Thus President Carter had no occasion to nominate a justice, but President Nixon appointed four. Secondly, even when a President appoints a judge he has no control over the justice's future decisions. Thus President Eisenhower was wont to say that appointing Chief Justice Warren and Justice Brennan constituted the two most serious mistakes of his presidency.

One case, of course, can hardly be conclusive evidence for or against judicial supremacy in constitutional matters. Privacy is perhaps an atypical right since it nowhere appears explicitly in the text of the constitutional document. It is a wholly judicial development. If anything is central to the US Bill of Rights, however, it is the First Amendment, which protects not only free speech but also the free exercise of religion. Another 1986 decision of the Supreme Court which therefore merits consideration is *Goldman* v. *Weinberger*. Goldman was an Orthodox Jew, a rabbi and a commissioned officer in the US Air Force, serving as a clinical psychologist at a mental health clinic on an air force base. He claimed that an air force regulation which prohibited the wearing of any headgear indoors infringed his First Amendment freedom to exercise his religious beliefs by wearing a yarmulka. A 5–4 majority decision rejected his claim. Rehnquist J. delivered the opinion of the Court on behalf of Burger CJ, White, Powell and Stevens JJ. Indignant dissents demonstrated the opposition of Brennan, Marshall, Blackmun and O'Connor JJ.

Justice Rehnquist was prepared to be deferential to the military. But he was so deferential that Justice Brennan, dissenting, described the majority as giving 'credulous deference to unsupported assertions of military necessity'. Thus Justice Rehnquist was convinced by the military's ploy of asking, 'Whatever next?' 'The government notes that while a yarmulka might not seem obtrusive to a Jew, neither does a turban to a Sikh, a saffron robe to a Satchidananda Yogi, nor dreadlocks to a Rastafarian.' This conjured up a rather implausible picture of the serried ranks of clinical psychologists at air force bases in California going to war in saffron robes or turbans. In the unlikely event that the fighting force's self-image and military discipline depended on Goldman's appearance, he would apparently have undermined his colleagues' morale by wearing a yarmulka but not, presumably, by wearing up to three rings and an identity bracelet, which air force regulations would have allowed.

Again, in reading the majority and the minority opinions, they seem to come from different worlds, or at least different centuries. The personalities and beliefs of the judges were clearly of far greater significance to the outcome of Goldman's case than was the wording of the First Amendment.

The difference made by personalities and political convictions can be illustrated in another way. 1973–4 was the last full term of the Supreme Court which saw both Justice Douglas, the Court's leading liberal, and Justice Rehnquist, the leading conservative, sitting together. There were 85 cases on civil rights, which at the risk of oversimplification we can categorise as disputes between an individual civil libertarian and the state. I am not presuming to comment on the strength of the cases one way or another. But it is striking that in 79 of these 85 cases Justice Douglas decided for the individual and in only 6 did he agree with the state, whereas Justice Rehnquist supported the state on 69 occasions and the individual on 16. Professor Abraham, one of the leading US constitutional scholars, adds this pertinent observation: 'Yet the two polar opposites heard the same cases, saw the same briefs and other documentation, took the same oath to the same constitution, were both superbly qualified students and scholars of the law.'*

Justice Douglas, the supreme liberal, had been confirmed

Justices and Presidents, 2nd ed., OUP, 1985, p. 317.

with only four votes against him in the Senate in 1939, when he had been described as 'a reactionary tool of Wall Street'! That supports my point about changes in the outlook of the appointee. Rehnquist, one of Nixon's appointments, had more difficulty in securing Senate confirmation, both as an Associate Justice and especially when President Reagan recently nominated him as the new Chief Justice. The Senate Judicial Committee's hearings deserve examination by those who advocate a British Bill of Rights. There were few questions about Rehnquist's legal skill. The thrust of the interrogation was instead concerned with his 'private' life and his political attitudes. Is that the way forward for the UK? Problems do not disappear just because a Bill of Rights is enacted. What happens is that judges, who interpret the Bill, take over from politicians as the decision-makers. But who appoints the judges? None other than the politicians in power. So those appointments then become a key political act. Judges are chosen according to a variety of factors, only one of which is their ability. Their political affiliations, their sex, their race, their religion, their friendship with the President, their geographical origins can all outweigh any deficiencies in their legal or judicial talents. Although President Reagan will be remembered for appointing the first woman justice in the history of the Supreme Court, 92 per cent of his appointments to the federal bench have been male, 98 per cent white and 98 per cent Republican.

A couple of 5–4 split decisions in the US Supreme Court do not detract from the glorious unanimous decision in *Brown*, nor from the Supreme Court's role in the US constitution. But they do remind us that those who interpret a Bill of Rights have great power which they can exercise in a variety of ways, not all of which will be to our liking. As the UK approaches the tercentennial celebrations of its own limited Bill of Rights, those who argue that we should incorporate the European Convention into our domestic law, and thus adopt a new Bill of Rights, must focus on who will interpret and apply the general language of that document.

The European Experience

One decision of the European Court of Human Rights stands out in the armoury of those who demand that we incorporate the Convention into our domestic law. Reference is made time after time to the *Sunday Times* thalidomide case. There the European Court ruled in 1979 that the English law of contempt of court, as laid down by the House of Lords in the 1974 case *Attorney-General* v. *Times Newspapers*, was in contravention of Article 10's guarantee of freedom of expression. This freed the *Sunday Times* to publish an article which was critical of Distillers, the manufacturer of the drug thalidomide. Although the European Court's ruling vindicated the newspaper's fight to publish, it came several years too late to influence the dispute between Distillers and the families affected by thalidomide. Supporters of incorporation praise the European Court for this critique of the English law and only bemoan the delay involved in taking a case such as this to Strasbourg. If we had had an incorporated Bill of Rights, they argue, English courts could have made that decision. But would they have done so? The Law Lords had considerable discretion as it was when they made their 1974 decision, which the European Court criticised. In a subsequent case, moreover, the House of Lords' majority repeated its restrictive approach, despite the European Court's decision. Statute law subsequently introduced the Strasbourg ruling into domestic law.

We should not get carried away by this example of a liberal decision by the European Court. It was by the narrowest of margins: 11–9. Nine European judges, then, were prepared to interpret the Convention so as to allow the Law Lords' decision to stand. The structure of the relevant Article is typical of the European Convention on Human Rights' drafting, and revealing of the latitude allowed to the interpreters:

Article 10
(1) Everyone has the right to freedom of expression. The

right shall include freedom to hold opinions and to receive and impart information and ideas without interference by public authority and regardless of frontiers. This Article shall not prevent States from requiring the licensing of broadcasting, television or cinema enterprises.

(2) The exercise of these freedoms, since it carries with it duties and responsibilities, may be subject to such formalities, conditions and restrictions or penalties as are prescribed by law and are necessary in a democratic society, in the interests of national security, territorial integrity or public safety, for the prevention of disorder or crime, for the protection of health or morals, for the protection of the reputation or rights of others, for preventing the disclosure of information received in confidence, or for maintaining the authority and impartiality of the judiciary.

Incorporating such an article into British law is not going to resolve anything in itself. Just like the eleven European judges in the majority or the nine in the minority, the interpreter has broad discretion as to how to balance the right against its many exceptions. Politicians and judges already make this kind of decision, albeit without explicitly acknowledging the trade-off. The important issues concern who has the decisive say and how they can be influenced. If Members of Parliament have the major role, at least they are exposed to the pressure of the media, the lobbyists and the interest groups and, more importantly, they are removable by the electorate. Moreover, they will often have the benefit of official reports and a great deal of briefing from departments, parties and unofficial researchers. Judges, in contrast, are deliberately insulated from pressure, are irremovable and decide on the very limited basis of what counsel for two parties in a particular dispute care to put before them. In the *Sunday Times* thalidomide case, one's natural sympathies are with those who suffered through thalidomide and with the campaigning newspaper, so the bare majority of the European Court came to what we would regard as the 'right' decision. It is understandable but hasty to claim that the European Convention is *therefore* a most desirable domestic Bill of Rights. For if one's only justification is that the European Court here achieved the 'right' balance, what if it sometimes gets the 'wrong' result, or if British judges would get the 'wrong' result?

To see how the European Convention on Human Rights is being interpreted today, let us consider the three most recent cases to receive wide publicity in the British press. We will reflect on three applications of the European Convention in the last few months: a trans-sexual's right to privacy; Irish citizens' rights to remarry; and trade unionists' right to freedom of association.

What exactly does it mean, for example, to say, as does Article 8 of the European Convention, that we have a right to respect for our private lives? The Article runs as follows:

(1) Everyone has the right to respect for his private and family life, his home and his correspondence.
(2) There shall be no interference by a public authority with the exercise of this right except such as is in accordance with the law and is necessary in a democratic society in the interests of national security, public safety or the economic well-being of the country, for the prevention of disorder or crime, for the protection of health or morals, or for the protection of the rights and freedoms of others.

The question in the recent Rees case was whether a trans-sexual's right to privacy was breached by the refusal of the Registrar-General to amend the trans-sexual's birth certificate. How would you interpret and apply Article 8 to this problem? There was considerable disagreement among the European institutions. The European Commission on Human Rights unanimously felt that Rees's right to privacy had been violated. But then the European Court of Human Rights, by twelve votes to three, decided that the Commission was wrong and that Article 8 had not been breached (see *The Times*, 21 October 1986). If the Commission and the Court are in such disagreement, perhaps we can conclude that privacy is a controversial right. Bills of Rights do not answer all the questions. Those who interpret the documents have great discretion and therefore power. How a British court would interpret the right to privacy is anyone's guess.

What about the absence of provision for divorce under Irish law? Does that contravene Article 8, set out above, or Article 12? The latter Article reads: 'Men and women of marriageable age have the right to marry and to found a family, according to the national laws governing the exercise of this right.' In *Johnston* v. *Republic of Ireland* (*The Times*, 7 January 1987) the Court dealt with a man who was formally separated from his wife and had been living with another woman for fifteen years. The Irish constitution prohibited divorce, so he was unable to divorce his wife in order to marry the woman with whom he now lived and had had a child. Again, how would you interpret Articles 8 and 12? The European Court, by sixteen votes to one, decided that Ireland's ban on divorce did not violate the Convention.

Our third example is the European Commission on Human Rights' consideration of the ban on trade unions at GCHQ, the government communications headquarters in Cheltenham. When the Law Lords decided that Mrs Thatcher was entitled to ban the unions without consultation, since she felt national security would be imperilled by negotiation, it was claimed in some quarters that this was the kind of case which would be decided differently if we had a Bill of Rights. Similarly, there are many misplaced expressions of confidence that the police raid on the BBC in Glasgow early in 1987, in connection with a television programme about the Zircon satellite, would have been condemned by judges interpreting a Bill of Rights. Yet there is little reason to suppose that judges who defer to claims of national security, as in the Law Lords' decision or in the granting of the Glasgow warrant, would somehow intervene more readily under the umbrella of a Bill of Rights. National security is, after all, an exception to the rights contained in the European Convention.

Sure enough, the European Commission rejected the GCHQ unions' claim that the ban on trade union membership at

GCHQ violated their right under Article 11 of the Convention. Thus the unions' case did not even reach the European Court, since it could not pass the first stage of convincing the Commission that there was a case to answer.

Lord Jowitt, then the Lord Chancellor, described the European Convention at the time of accepting it in 1950 as 'so vague and woolly that it may mean almost anything'. To be more precise, it will mean whatever its interpreters want it to mean. Of course, whether or not we have a domestic Bill of Rights, we will still be subject to the European institutions' interpretation of the Convention. But the Court does tend to allow what it calls a 'margin of appreciation' to national laws, so it is essential to decide whether the final word on the domestic interpretation should come from Parliament or the courts. Even an unentrenched domestic Bill of Rights would, in practice, shift that power away from Parliament (which would be reluctant to be seen to be legislating 'contrary to the Bill of Rights' even if it technically could do so) and towards the judges. Is that really desirable?

British Implications

It could be argued that we already defer to the European Court of Human Rights, so should we not allow British judges the same power to review our law in the light of the European Convention, instead of suffering the allegedly humiliating spectacle of washing our dirty linen in public at Strasbourg? This argument, often put forward by the tumble-drying classes who have no idea of washing laundry in public, is flawed. The origin of the European Convention was the idea of the Western European democracies watching each other in front of the public of Europe to guard against a repeat of fascism's abuses of human rights. Anyone who watches *EastEnders* will know that the launderette is a place not only to wash dirty linen but also to exchange ideas. It is central to the development of community values.

But is the analogy with European judges really apt? There is a considerable difference between twenty-one European judges, one from each country, interpreting a vague document and one, three or five British judges having the same power. This is not a criticism of our own judges. It is, rather, an acknowledgement of two facts. Firstly, the full European Court brings a breadth of experience and a variety of traditions which cannot be matched by a small group of British judges. Secondly, no single, transient British government can turn a majority of the European Court. But any one government can and usually does influence the make-up of Britain's judiciary. Lord Hailsham, the Lord Chancellor, and Mrs Thatcher have nominated all the senior judges bar one during the period since 1979. They have done that without seeking to shift the courts significantly to the right. But could they, or any other government, be so self-effacing if judges were yet more powerful? Would we not expect that the more powerful the courts became, the more pressure there would be to appoint sympathetic judges? As the US experience shows, this does not always work to the satisfaction of those who appoint. Judges sometimes confound the expectations of those who choose them. We would nevertheless slide down the road to US-style nominations, based on political ideology, and confirmation hearings. Is that the route we want to travel?

The trouble with enacting a Bill of Rights, therefore, is that it sets us on an uncertain constitutional path. It might lead to great gains in our civil liberties, but it might not. It will certainly alter the nature of appointments to the judiciary. This may be a consummation devoutly to be wished, but we need to know what the new system of appointing judges would be. Although the present Lord Chancellor is in favour of a Bill of Rights, he is not in favour of any reforms in the method of appointing judges. He would like to keep this within his control. However, the corollary of a Bill of Rights would surely be a Minister of Justice in the Commons, who would have to account to a Select Committee for his nominations to the Bench. One change in the constitution inevitably leads on to other reforms, and how can we be confident that the end result is preferable to the present arrangements? We cannot. Why therefore should we take a leap in the dark? We should not.

Irrespective of questions about the judges, it is difficult to believe that British court procedure is the best environment for a thorough analysis of such problematic political questions as the Bill would give them. Why should an adversarial dispute between two parties, largely argued on the basis of precedent, be the forum in which to decide, for instance, whether a Labour government's proposals against private education or in favour of re-nationalisation offend the First Protocol to the European Convention?

We are a long way off the kind of procedure which Americans and others would associate with courts interpreting a Bill of Rights. We have not yet mastered the art of lawyers filing briefs as *amici curiae*, 'friends of the court'. We have not yet mastered the idea of Brandeis briefs, in which a full range of social and economic evidence about the likely consequences of alternative judicial conclusions is put to the judges. We have not yet adopted the US practice of assigning the best young lawyers to act as clerks or research assistants to the judges. We have not yet adopted the European Community's equivalent of using more experienced lawyers to act as *référendaires* to the European Court of Justice (a different entity from the European Court of Human Rights; the former applies Community law in Luxembourg, the latter Convention law in Strasbourg). One might expect some of these developments to emerge once we had a Bill of Rights, but it would be more reassuring if we were shown, in advance, some commitment by the legal professions to reform our court procedures in order to fulfil different and broader duties.

If, contrary to my argument, judges are to pull the constitutional strings in the future, we should hasten to prepare lawyers for that wide-ranging task. We will have to shake up our court procedure and think seriously about the qualifications for judicial service. Judge Learned Hand, the

eminent US lawyer who was sadly denied the chance to grace
the Supreme Court himself, described the magnitude and
latitude of the formidable task we would be assigning to
judges:

> I venture to believe that it is as important to a judge
> called upon to pass on a question of constitutional law,
> to have a bowing acquaintance with Acton and Maitland,
> with Thucydides, Gibbon, and Carlyle, with Homer,
> Dante, Shakespeare, and Milton, with Machiavelli,
> Montaigne, and Rabelais, with Plato, Bacon, Hume and
> Kant, as with books that have been specifically written
> on the subject. For in such matters everything turns
> upon the spirit in which he approaches the question
> before him. The words he must construe are empty
> vessels into which he can pour nearly everything he
> will. Men do not gather figs of thistles, nor supply
> institutions from judges whose outlook is limited by
> parish or class. They must be aware that there are before
> them more than verbal problems; more than final
> solutions cast in generalisations of universal applic-
> ability. They must be aware of the changing social
> tensions in every society which make it an organism;
> which demand new schemata of adaptation; which will
> disrupt it, if rigidly confined.*

Those who argue that such a job description indicates the
enormous power of judges who act as constitutional guardians might well put their faith instead in those who exercise
ultimate power in society being removable through elections
and accountable through public argument. In British practice
this means politicians not judges. Thus the leftist argument
against a Bill of Rights is, in essence, that politics is about
power, that this should not be obscured by legal form and that
the power should not be exercised by irremovable and
unaccountable judges. This is not a complacent argument. On

---

*Learned Hand, *The Spirit of Liberty*, ed. I. Dilliard, New York, 1952.

the contrary, it demands reform of a different kind. As
Professor John Griffith has argued:

> I believe firmly that political decisions should be taken
> by politicians. In a society like ours this means by people
> who are removable. It is an obvious corollary of this that
> the responsibility and accountability of our rulers
> should be real and not fictitious. And of course our
> existing institutions, especially the House of Commons,
> need strengthening. And we need to force governments
> out into the open. So also the freedom of the press
> should be enlarged by the amendment of laws which
> restrict discussion.*

A Constitutional Council

All the above discussion points in the direction of resisting
the adoption of a Bill of Rights which would be enforceable
in the courts. But there is a better solution. Judges are not the
only possible interpreters of a Bill of Rights. If we have
enough imagination to challenge the existing constitutional
order, why stop at introducing broad guarantees of rights?
Let's think seriously about the guardians of such rights.
Should we entrust such power to selected lawyers, however
distinguished in their own profession? Or should we opt for a
Constitutional Committee of the Privy Council which would
have a broader composition, perhaps along the lines of the
French Conseil Constitutionnel?

In a Fabian paper in 1968, Anthony Lester QC began the
movement for a new British Bill of Rights by calling for the
incorporation of the European Convention on Human Rights
but at that time he favoured making it unenforceable in the
courts. Although he now supports the enforcement of a Bill of

---

* 'The Political Constitution', *The Modern Law Review* (42), 1979, p. 16.

Rights through the courts, he then thought that instead of transferring power to judges we should create a Constitutional Council which could make recommendations to Parliament about the compatibility with the Bill of Rights of legislative or executive action (or, I would add, legislative or executive inaction and the inadequacies of the common law). I would suggest a Constitutional Committee of the Privy Council, consisting of not only the senior judges but also senior statesmen and perhaps augmented by the kind of people who head Royal Commissions and Committees of Inquiry (Williams, Warnock, Blake, Bullock, Quinton) and also some wise people from a wider base than these members of the 'great and good' who head Oxbridge colleges.

Such a body could be modelled on the French Conseil Constitutionnel. It would have certain advantages over a court, namely a broader composition, the opportunity to consider matters in advance and surmounting the objections of opponents that any such Bill will have indeterminable, and possibly harmful, consequences for the judiciary. The idea of a Constitutional Council would fit in well with the Law Commission and the increasingly impressive system of Select Committees. It would not be a barrier to the eventual decision to make the European Convention directly enforceable. Indeed, it could usefully examine the ramifications of creating a Constitutional Court. If the real motive for the Bill of Rights movement is the promotion of human rights, and the real motive for objection is the danger of yet more politicisation of the judiciary, then a Constitutional Council deserves serious consideration by both sides. It is not enough to campaign for a Bill of Rights without answering the objections. It is not enough to object without providing another answer to those who question the protection of civil liberties under current arrangements.

Limits of Law

Nor is it enough to expect constitutional reform to safeguard our rights on its own. As the Weimar Republic showed, a perfect paper constitution is not an adequate protection of civil liberties. It is an impoverished vision of the human condition which thinks only of changing institutions and laws. We best protect rights by changing attitudes.

This lesson has recently been learnt by the government and by various charities. As 1986 gave way to 1987, three pressing social problems were addressed in a constructive way through advertising and without the Pavlovian response of recourse to law. The curse of drunken driving, the curse of AIDS and the curse of homelessness are three problems we will doubtless face for the rest of the century. None would be helped by a domestic Bill of Rights. But the government advertisements in relation to the first two and the campaign (headed by Lord Scarman, the major inspiration for a Bill of Rights in the UK) for the International Year of Shelter for the Homeless have been asking us persuasively not to stand on our legal rights but to do something above and beyond what the law requires us to do. The call is for people to forgo their legal rights: we are legally entitled to drive even after we have drunk alcohol; we have the legal right to be promiscuous; and we have the legal right to walk past on the other side while the homeless shiver. But nobody could pretend that the legal rights alone are what matters. We must not shelter behind the law's minimal demands and forget our moral responsibilities.

Similarly, we should not be lulled by the prospect of a Bill of Rights into believing that paper rights can safeguard our civil liberties. We have already returned to the leftist argument that politics, including claims for rights, rest on power. Now we come back to the rightist argument that we need to conserve our cultural scepticism of those in power, we need to develop our personal responsibility for civil liberties, we should not regard a Bill of Rights as much more than a diversion from the real safeguard for our liberties. And that safeguard is our own attitude. The price of liberty, as Curran's aphorism reminds us, is eternal vigilance.

Just as the political right could agree with the left on the need to have power where we can see it and to exercise some control over it, so the left could agree with the right on this final point, that attitudes are more important than legal form. The point was well put by that liberal judge on whose wisdom we have already relied, Learned Hand:

> I often wonder whether we do not rest our hopes too much upon constitutions, upon laws and upon courts. These are false hopes; believe me, these are false hopes. Liberty lies in the hearts of men and women; when it dies there no constitution, no law, no court can save it; no constitution, no law, no court can even do much to help it. While it lies there it needs no constitution, no law, no court to save it.*

The same message was delivered by Professor Grant Gilmore, who concluded his summary of *The Ages of American Law*† with a note of caution. Undoubtedly the US Bill of Rights has been used to good effect, particularly the 'due process' clause of its Fourteenth Amendment. But even its greatest supporters would echo Learned Hand's warning. Thus Professor Gilmore leaves us with the following speculation: 'In heaven there will be no law, and the lion will lie down with the lamb. . . . In hell there will be nothing but law, and due process will be meticulously observed.' The path to hell is paved with good intentions, such as the good faith of those who argue for a UK Bill of Rights. I do not claim that such a development would lead us down the road to hell but neither do I believe that a Bill of Rights would take us straight to heaven. The less glamorous truth is probably that the way forward for those who value civil liberties involves a lot of hard work in purgatory.

---

*Learned Hand, op. cit.
†Yale University Press, 1977.

Endpiece

Julia Neuberger

There now exists an inchoate, barely articulated mood for a greater degree of individual liberty and individual say, which may be the political effect of greater economic independence which many feel they now enjoy. Such a mood may well cut against the old Labour corporatist values as well as new right authoritarianism, and it can be uncomfortable for the left: it is not one that the left can ignore or suppress.*

A New National Mood?

On 6 February 1987 Sir Edward Gardner's Bill failed by just six votes to get its second reading in the House of Commons. It was a modest Bill, designed to incorporate into British law the European Convention on Human Rights. Since it is a Convention to which Britain is already party, and since British citizens already have the right of individual appeal to the European Court of Human Rights in Strasbourg, the whole issue may seem to many to be a great fuss about nothing. Yet it arouses strong passions among specific groups. The Zircon spy satellite affair revealed considerable respect for libertarian values in unexpected places. There are signs of unease across the political spectrum, and even among people who are apolitical, caused by the perceived increasing power and authoritarianism of the state and of the big corporations.

---

*Editorial, *New Statesman*, 13 February 1987.

Two issues are addressed in this book, separate but inextricably bound together in philosophical terms. The issue of a Bill of Rights concerns the protection of specific individual human rights against the state and against big business. It can be seen as part of a desire for major constitutional reform. The question of a Freedom of Information Act is also about the rights of the individual against the state and big business, but it is largely concerned with official secrecy, particularly the debate about the abolition of Section 2 of the Official Secrets Act. The desire to enact either a Bill of Rights or a Freedom of Information Act is seen as a 'liberal-democratic approach' to constitutional reform. 'Although liberal-democratic diagnoses of the national disease, and prescriptions for treatment, are not identical', those who fall into this camp 'agree in principle that what is needed is a set of reforms that would submit politicians, of whatever party, to more and stronger checks of a legal and political nature than at present'.*

Both a Bill of Rights and a Freedom of Information Act are crucial aspects of the SDP/Liberal Alliance's programme of constitutional reform. Indeed, the Alliance is frequently accused of being interested in not much else! Austin Mitchell, Labour MP for Great Grimsby, sees in such proposed reforms the prospects of a major political change in Britain, which he feels the Labour Party has been slow to accept:

> As the people . . . achieve a certain level of well-being and independence they become less keen on being handed things, more irritated by the 'nanny' state. They want to choose, to be involved, to feel they are heard on government, the environment, local matters and at work. . . . They are choosing as consumers. . . . Other parties have seen the change; the need to make govern-ment a political version of the Consumers' Association. The Alliance have made such a fetish of it that they have

---

*Dawn Oliver, 'Constitutional Reform: Means and Ends', *Current Legal Problems*, 1986.

nothing else to offer. The New Zealand Labour Party
promised, and is painfully delivering, a Bill of Rights.*

Is a genuine change taking place in Britain in this field? If so,
when does it date from? Are all the political parties likely to
take it on board, or are there such strong objections to some of
the proposed measures, even those which have a fair measure
of all-party support, that Conservatives and Labour in office or
in opposition could never see themselves supporting these
proposals? To understand something of this debate, it is
necessary to go back to the decision of the UK to become party
to the European Convention on Human Rights.

The UK and the European Convention

In 1950 the Council of Europe adopted the European
Convention for the Protection of Human Rights and
Fundamental Freedoms (usually referred to as the European
Convention on Human Rights and abbreviated to ECHR). The
UK played a major role in this; the draftsman was Sir Oscar
Dowson, a former senior legal adviser at the Home Office, and
Sir David Maxwell-Fyffe (later Lord Chancellor Kilmuir)
played a major role as chairman of the Consultative Assembly's
legal committee. Anthony Lester's F. A. Mann Lecture, later
published in *Public Law*,† records the exchanges between
ministers at the time and shows that the project had the
support of the Foreign Secretary, Ernest Bevin, and his
Minister of State, Kenneth Younger, and was opposed by Lord
Chancellor Jowitt, Colonial Secretary James Griffiths and
by Chancellor of the Exchequer Sir Stafford Cripps. In the
European Consultative Assembly the Convention was sup-

---

*'New Rights Diary', *New Statesman*, 13 February 1987.
†Spring 1984.

ported by Sir Winston Churchill, Harold Macmillan and John Foster for the Conservatives, by Lord Layton for the Liberals and by Lynn Ungoed-Thomas QC for Labour.

The main objection to the proposal seems to have been to the suggestion that individuals should have the right to petition the European Commission directly. In fact the right of individual petition was made voluntary at that time. The Convention was signed by the Committee of Ministers of the Council of Europe on 4 November 1950, and the UK became the first state to ratify the Convention, on 18 March 1951.

All this has to be seen against a background of pan-European horror at what had happened to the Jews, gypsies, homosexuals, left-wingers and other objectors in Nazi Europe. It came shortly after the Nuremberg trials, and the scale of the horror left many European politicians with a view that the protection of human rights on a Europe-wide basis was a matter of urgency. Basic concern can be seen from the Article 14 of the Convention, which guarantees all the other rights and freedoms in the Convention without unfair discrimination: 'The enjoyment of the rights and freedoms set forth in this Convention shall be secured without discrimination on any ground such as sex, race, colour, language, religion, political or other opinion, national or social origin, association with a national minority, property, birth or other status.'

The UK, having ratified the Convention, then proceeded to extend it to forty-two overseas territories for which it was responsible in 1953. By 1957 it was agreed that fundamental rights should be included in the constitution of the new state of Nigeria, and clauses modelled on the European Convention became part of the Nigerian constitution of 1960. As both Anthony Lester QC and Professor Michael Zander point out in detail, there were then twenty-four Commonwealth countries into whose independence constitutions the Convention was transplanted.* Anthony Lester observed: 'The Parliament of Westminster has thus exported the fundamental rights and freedoms of the Convention to the new Commonwealth on a

---

*Michael Zander, *A Bill of Rights?*, Sweet & Maxwell, 1985, p. 29.

scale without parallel in the rest of the world.'*

In 1960 the federal parliament of Canada enacted a statute entitled the Canadian Bill of Rights, and the Westminster Parliament, in 1982, in passing the Canada Act, enacted 'a modern, strong and comprehensive Charter of Fundamental Rights', modelled at least partly on the US Bill of Rights.

In 1948 the United Nations decided to adopt the Universal Declaration of Human Rights by 48 votes to none. Although the Declaration is not legally binding, it is generally regarded as an important statement of principle. It deals with wider issues than the European Convention, since it covers political, civil, economic and social rights. In particular it covers social security, the right to work, equal pay, just remuneration and public assistance with housing. This is significant because one of the many objections to the incorporation of the European Convention on Human Rights into British law comes from those on the political left, who point to the absence of the right to work, for instance, from the rights and freedoms guaranteed within it. Simon Lee, in his contribution to this book, advances this argument when he says that there is no general prohibition on discrimination (other than in the rights and freedoms guaranteed by the ECHR), so that discrimination in employment would not be covered by a Bill of Rights incorporating the European Convention. Similarly, the New Statesman's editorial of 13 February 1987 comments: 'Within the left, more attention is now being focused on the question of real economic rights – to an income, to a job, to social benefits – as the necessary underpinning for real freedom.'

The Idea of Human Rights

Where do these ideas of rights come from? They have a long history. The great English philosophers John Locke

---

*F.A. Mann Lecture, Public Law, Spring 1984, pp. 56–7.

(1632–1704) and John Stuart Mill (1806–73) argued that men (women were not included at this time, although Mill did address himself to some of those issues later) had a right to certain liberties. For example, Locke writes on equality:

> A state also of equality, wherein all the power and jurisdiction is reciprocal, no one having more than another; there being nothing more evident than that creatures of the same species and rank . . . should also be equal one amongst another without subordination or subjection. . . . But though this [the state of nature] be a state of liberty, yet it is not a state of licence; though man . . . has an uncontrollable liberty to dispose of his person or possessions, yet he has not liberty to destroy himself. . . . No one ought to harm another in his life, health, liberty or possessions.*

Locke and the French philosopher Rousseau did much to create the philosophical climate in which the French and American revolutions took place. On 4 July 1776 the Continental Congress in Philadelphia adopted the American Declaration of Independence, proclaiming it as a self-evident truth that 'all men are created equal, that they are endowed by their Creator with certain unalienable Rights, that among these are Life, Liberty, and the pursuit of Happiness'. Two centuries later, Judge Pollak observed:

> By tracing these rights to the 'Creator' and by characterising them as 'unalienable', the Declaration gave important impetus to the principle – which also had its antecedents in Locke's writings – that some individual rights exist in perpetuity apart from and above the laws periodically prescribed by particular kings and legislatures vested transiently with the power to govern.†

---

*Quoted in Bertrand Russell, *A History of Western Philosophy*, Allen & Unwin, 1961, p. 603.
†L. H. Pollak, *The Constitution and the Supreme Court*, Vol. 1, Meridian Books, USA, 1968, p. 18.

These rights were beyond humanity; they came of divine authority, as described in the American Declaration. This is important, for many of the objections to Bills of Rights – or, indeed, to the concept of human rights as against human responsibilities (an issue constantly raised, which will be addressed later) – focus even now on human duty to perform certain things, on human responsibilities to obey God's and human law. The idea of 'rights' is said to be an anti-religious, eighteenth-century-rationalist, quasi-revolutionary concept. When the French revolutionary government of 1791 adopted the French Declaration of the Rights of Man and the Citizen, another English commentator, Jeremy Bentham, attacked the doctrine as so much 'bawling upon paper' and as 'nonsense upon stilts'. As Anthony Lester puts it: 'British constitutional thinkers since Bentham have continued to pour scorn both upon the doctrine and its translation into the legal guarantees of the American Bill of Rights.'*

The idea was nevertheless contagious, spreading with Napoleon through Europe and with the movement for independence to the British Empire and Commonwealth overseas. The doctrine of human rights became increasingly refined, particularly as new Bills of Rights and statements became legally enforceable. Constitutional lawyers and legal philosophers devoted a considerable amount of their energies to discussion of the matter, mainly in the USA but also in Europe. Britain lagged behind in many ways, since until comparatively recently the issue was not seen as being of major importance.

A. V. Dicey's views on the matter have shaped British constitutional thinking for a hundred years, and it may be due to him that at least part of the issue was not taken seriously. For he argued hard for 'the absolute legislative sovereignty or despotism of the King in Parliament'. The implication is that there is no supreme law which tests the validity of other laws in Britain. Parliament has sovereignty; it can do what it likes.

---

*Public Law, Spring 1984, p. 48.

Concepts such as the American one, of individual citizens being divinely endowed with unalienable rights which Parliament cannot take away, are foreign to Dicey's thinking. His view of the constitution relies on a system of completely impartial judges who will apply the law as Parliament has made it, but who will be in no sense political. Inherent in this thinking is also a scepticism about the value of written guarantees in the shape of constitutions. This point is frequently made by opponents of a UK Bill of Rights, who point for example to Amin's Uganda, where there was a perfectly good Bill of Rights but it was of no value in the protection of human life or property.

Human Rights and Human Duties

Discussion about the nature of human rights continues. Before returning to the domestic debate about a UK Bill of Rights, it is worth considering how the issue has been argued in the United States throughout the twentieth century and before as to what precisely these liberties, or rights, are. In recent years John Rawls, a US political philosopher who has been influential on the liberal left on both sides of the Atlantic, has suggested that individuals have rights, not to certain liberties as Locke and Mill thought they did, but to equal respect and concern in the design of political institutions. Rawls argues for a liberal constitution in order to achieve the fundamental right to equality. He suggests that people would protect the basic liberties, once a certain level of material wealth had been reached, because they would understand that a threat to self-respect, which the basic liberties protect, becomes the most serious threat to equal respect.*

Ronald Dworkin has commented in considerable detail on

*J. Rawls, *A Theory of Justice*, Oxford University Press, 1973.

Rawls's ideas. He traces the intellectual history of political theories, which he divides into goal-based, right-based and duty-based theories. He argues that goal-based theories have as their aim the achievement of some fundamental goal, such as the greatest good of the greatest number, or general welfare. They are not concerned with the welfare of the individual except in so far as he or she contributes to that specific aim. This, Dworkin argues, is true of fascism, which takes the interests and aims of a specific political organisation as fundamental. More contentiously, he says that it is also true of utilitarianism:

> because, though they count up the impact of political decisions on distinct individuals, and are in this way concerned with individual welfare, they merge these impacts into overall totals or averages and take the improvement of these laws or averages as desirable quite apart from the decision of any individual that it is.*

Dworkin then contrasts this type of thinking with the two other possibilities, right-based and duty-based theories, and argues that both of these put the individual at the centre and take the individual's decision or conduct as being of fundamental importance. But they differ in how they regard the individual:

> Duty-based theories are concerned with the moral quality of his acts, because they suppose that it is wrong . . . for an individual to fail to meet certain standards of behaviour. . . . Right-based theories are, in contrast, concerned with the independence rather than the conformity of individual action. They presuppose and protect the value of individual thought and choice. Both types of theory make use of the idea of moral rules, codes of conduct to be followed, on individual occasions, without consulting self-interest.†

---

*R. Dworkin, *Taking Rights Seriously*, Duckworth, 1977, p. 172.
†Ibid.

He then goes on to argue that duty-based theories require an individual to conform to whatever code of conduct is generally accepted, while right-based theories imply the codes of conduct are instrumental, necessary to protect the rights of others, but have no inherent value in themselves.

This is somewhat superficial and oversimplified, as Professor Dworkin admits. It nevertheless explains the strong reaction of many fundamentalist religious groups to the idea of 'rights'. If it is true that no inherent value is to be found in the code of conduct which ensures those rights, but that it is merely an instrument for achieving an aim, then those religious groups that argue for the divinity of their scriptures and for the individual's duty to perform the religious obligations spelled out in those scriptures are going to take considerable offence. For they would argue, as many Jewish authorities have done, that religious law is about our duty to obey God's law, which will result in the best of all possible worlds (although that is not the reason for doing it), and not about our inherent rights as humans. However, Haim Cohn, once Supreme Court Justice in Israel, neatly points out that the individual's duty to do something implies a collateral right of someone else to have the duty done. He cites, for instance, the divine command to give charity; that duty must imply the right of the poor person to receive charity.* The same logic can be used to refute fundamentalist Christian and Islamic opponents of the human rights idea. But the argument about duties rather than rights is increasing. Within the USA, one of the crucial components of the 'rights' doctrine has been the assertion that the rights are themselves divinely endowed, imposing a duty upon individuals to ensure that other individuals have those rights respected.

---

*H. Cohn, *Human Rights in Jewish Law*, Ktav Publishing (USA), 1984, p. 18.

The UK Bill of Rights Debate

As yet the argument in Britain has not on the whole been of the rights-versus-duties variety. In this book Simon Lee mentions the argument but does not use it. His objections are different and much more in line with the traditional objections to a UK Bill of Rights. The debate started in earnest in Britain, as distinct from the ratification of the European Convention and the granting of individual rights to appeal to it in 1965, less than twenty years ago. In 1968 Anthony Lester wrote a pamphlet entitled *Democracy and Individual Rights.** He put forward the view that the individual was under threat from a variety of sources, including Parliament, the Civil Service, local government and 'those clusters of private, oligarchical power which compete with government in significance and scale'. Lester argued that Parliament had occasionally reacted to popular prejudice against a minority, and cited several instances. One was the Aliens Act 1905, passed to assuage fears of 'being swamped' by Jews from Eastern Europe who were fleeing pogroms. The Aliens Act of 1914 was even worse, a reaction to war hysteria that passed through all its parliamentary stages in a single day. Both these statutes were passed as emergency Acts yet both were still in force in 1968. There were also the Commonwealth Immigrants Act of 1962, 1965 and 1968, the last of which had gone through all its stages in the space of a week.

Lester's further and more significant example of the denial of individual freedoms by Parliament was the delegation to the executive of sweeping arbitrary powers. One instance was the delegation of wide-ranging powers to an immigration official under the Aliens Act. Another was the system of security tests for government employees accused of some breach; they cannot be represented, nor are they entitled to know the evidence against them. There were many other

---

*Fabian Society tract No. 390.

examples, which led Lester to propose the enacting of a Bill of Rights which could not be enforced by the courts but would have primarily an educational function. That Bill of Rights was to be the European Convention.

The proposal was sporadically, and not always adequately, debated over the next few years, in Parliament and outside. In 1969 Lord Lambton (Conservative) sought leave to introduce a ten-minute-rule Bill 'to preserve the rights of the individual'. He was opposed by Alex Lyon (Labour); the debate lasted fourteen minutes, and no one else spoke. In 1969, however, John Macdonald, then chairman of the Liberal Lawyers, wrote a pamphlet entitled *A Bill of Rights* which went further than Anthony Lester's. He argued that a Bill of Rights had to be enforceable in the ordinary courts and that the need for such protection arose from various causes, such as the growth of bureaucracy, the new threats to privacy from the computer and from telephone tapping and the increased concentration of power in Whitehall. John Macdonald drafted a Bill which gave rights in twenty-four specific areas, and in June 1969 Lord Wade started a four-hour debate on the proposals in the House of Lords. In July 1969 Emlyn Hooson QC raised the issue in the Commons. Perhaps more surprisingly, also in 1969 the then Quintin Hogg MP (now Lord Hailsham), opposition front-bench spokesman on Home Office affairs, published (through the Conservative Central Office) a pamphlet representing his own views. Hogg argued the need for constitutional reform and for a Human Rights Bill of some sort. However, less than two years later, back in the House of Lords, Lord Hailsham had changed his mind; he opposed Lord Arran's Bill of Rights, since he had basic difficulties accepting a Bill of Rights of any kind.

The debate continued. Sam Silkin QC moved the second reading of a Protection of Human Rights Bill in 1971. There was so little interest among MPs that the House was counted out for lack of forty Members present.

Interest was revived when Sir Leslie Scarman gave his Hamlyn Lectures in December 1974. Scarman argued that English law was facing a crisis from the pressure of the international human rights movement; both the United Nations General Assembly's Universal Declaration of Human Rights and the more recent European Convention, he said, 'reflect a rising tide of opinion, which, in one way or another, will have to be accommodated in the English legal system'. He saw its difficulties: 'Charters, constitutions, broadly generalised declarations of rights, just do not fit. We have no written constitution.' And he took seriously objections on the basis that human rights were already protected in English law:

> The point is a fair one: and deserves to be taken seriously. When times are normal and fear is not stalking the land, English law sturdily protects the freedom of the individual and respects human personality. But when times are abnormally alive with fear and prejudice, the common law is at a disadvantage: it cannot resist the will, however frightened and prejudiced it may be, of Parliament.

Scarman reasoned that it was the helplessness of the law in the face of the legislative sovereignty of Parliament which made it difficult for the legal system to accommodate the concept of fundamental and inviolable human rights. He was convinced that the means had to be found for a declaration of these rights to be incorporated into British law and for those rights to be protected from any encroachment, including by the power of the state.

Scarman's appeal was picked up by politicians across the spectrum. Sir Keith Joseph entered the fray in 1975. Lord Hailsham changed his mind again and decided that something needed to be done. James Kilfedder (Ulster Unionist) proposed the setting up of a Royal Commission to investigate the Bill of Rights idea, and Alan Beith introduced a Bill of Rights Bill in July 1975. The Labour Party joined in, too, with the publication of a discussion paper (the party's Home Policy Committee and National Executive would not allow it to be policy): *Charter of Human Rights*, by the Human Rights Subcommittee of the Home Policy Committee of the National Executive. Only three days before publication, Roy Jenkins, then Labour Home Secretary, argued that he, too, was moving towards the idea of incorporating the European Convention on Human Rights into UK law.

In March 1976 Lord Wade moved a debate in the House of Lords on a fresh Bill designed to incorporate the European Convention into UK law. The House gave that Bill an unopposed second reading, although both Lord Hailsham and Lord Lloyd had registered strong objections. Throughout 1977 and 1978 the campaign continued. The Conservative front bench had decided to support it, at least in the context of the devolution legislation. The House of Lords set up a Select Committee on a Bill of Rights, after a debate in February 1977, initiated yet again by the indefatigable Lord Wade. The committee reported in November 1978 that 'in any country, whatever its constitution, the existence or absence of legislation in the nature of a Bill of Rights could in practice only play a relatively minor part in the protection of human rights. What was important above all was a country's political climate and traditions.'* The chairman of the Select Committee, Lord Allen of Abbeydale, opened the debate and moved that the House take note of the report. But Lord Wade moved an amendment urging the government 'to introduce a Bill of Rights to incorporate the European Convention on Human Rights into the domestic law of the United Kingdom'. The amendment was carried by 56 votes to 30.

Since 1978 the campaign to secure the incorporation of the European Convention on Human Rights into British law has continued. In 1979 Lord Wade again introduced his Bill. It was passed by the Lords again but not even considered by the Commons. In 1981 the Bill was debated and defeated in the Commons. In 1983 Robert Maclennan MP (Social Democrat) introduced a European Human Rights Convention Bill under the ten-minute rule; there was no debate, and the Bill lapsed. But in June 1984, 107 Conservative MPs signed an early-day motion calling for the incorporation of the European Conven-

---

*Michael Zander, *A Bill of Rights?*, Sweet & Maxwell, 1985, p. 24.

tion into British law, and in 1985 Lord Scarman himself introduced a Bill in the Lords to incorporate the Convention. Lord Broxbourne did the same in 1986, and Sir Edward Gardner introduced a Bill in the Commons in February 1987. The campaign is still rolling.

Michael Zander has argued strongly for the incorporation of the European Convention into British law, citing many of the cases where the UK has found itself in the dock at Strasbourg to advance two arguments. One is that there is no adequate protection of human rights and fundamental freedoms in the UK, and the other is that the nation is constantly having its dirty linen washed in public at Strasbourg. Simon Lee, apart from criticising the European Convention for what it does not contain, and therefore likewise the proposed UK Bill of Rights (assuming that the incorporation of the ECHR is the only realistic present possibility) takes a different line. He regards it not as a pro-and-con argument but as 'a question of attitude, style and emphasis, of political, legal and constitutional culture'. He believes that we must consider the kind of society Britain would become with a Bill of Rights and compare that with the society we are and would like to be. Lee addresses the question of whether Britain has no constitution, as many of the proponents of a Bill of Rights, Michael Zander and Lord Scarman among them, would maintain. He concludes that the definition is wrong, and that one way or another we do have a constitution.

It depends on what one means by 'constitution'. Simon Lee points to the 'good chaps theory of government' as practised in the UK, saying that we can rely on the consciences and need for re-election of our politicians to ensure their 'good behaviour'. These, he suggests, are the two safeguards against politicians' abuse of their 'theoretically unlimited power'. Against this must be weighed Anthony Lester's examples of panic actions by Parliament against aliens in the early years of the century and against Commonwealth immigrants in the 1960s. Where then were the consciences? Or do they take second place to the desire to be re-elected, pandering to public prejudices? Simon Lee recognises the 'good chaps theory of government' as the conservative position, the desire to retain the status quo. Lord Hailsham, the present Lord Chancellor, supports a Bill of Rights but does not support reform in the appointment of judges, which is done directly by him. Lee asks whether a Bill of Rights does not presuppose some other kind of constitutional reform, including the setting up of a Ministry of Justice, accountable to a Select Committee over the appointing of the judiciary.

Lee is concerned whether the judiciary as at present constituted (and arguably as they might exist under another system, since he is unconvinced that such changes would be beneficial) should have the say over constitutional issues. Judges are not removable, while politicians are. The leftist argument against a Bill of Rights is, he says, 'that politics is about power, that this should not be obscured by legal form and that the power should not be exercised by irremovable and unaccountable judges'.

Michael Zander disagrees. He believes that policy issues have always been addressed by the judges in some way, that English procedure needs some reform if it is to be more effective and that 'there is still a major creative function for the judges'. The importance of the judicial role is, he says, concealed by the judges' tendency to proclaim that what they are doing is no more than stating what the law *is*. Judges do not admit that their role includes an element of saying what the law ought to be. Later on Zander argues that 'Policy issues are . . . and always have been part of judicial decision-making.' The question then has to be whether having a Bill of Rights would give an unwelcome boost to judicial policy-making, unelected as the judges are.

It was a curious coincidence – or perhaps no coincidence at all – that the 1986 Reith Lectures were given by Lord McCluskey, a Scots High Court judge who was Solicitor-General for Scotland under two Labour administrations. McCluskey also takes the view that the judges should not be drawn into the policy-making area:

And that's just the problem with a constitutional Bill of

Rights. It is inevitably a charter of enduring super-rights, rights written in delphic words but in indelible ink on an opaque surface. It turns judges into legislators and gives them a finality which our whole tradition has hitherto professed to withhold from them. It makes the mistake of dressing up policy choices as if they were legal choices. It asks those whose job it is to know and apply the law to create and reform the law. It requires those whose skill it is to know what the law is to decide what it should be. If the legislature shirks the task of deciding what the law should be, either by avoiding the issue altogether, as it sometimes does, or by addressing the issue but refusing to make the essential detailed policy choices, the judges are compelled to step into the breach. Judges abhor a legal vacuum. So if legislators or constitution-makers pronounce resoundingly that 'All men are equal' but fail to indicate whether 'men' includes or excludes women, slaves, blacks, aliens or unborn foetuses or corporate persons, then judges have to decide. . . . Those who interpret a constitution cannot avoid choosing among competing social and political visions. The walls between the political and judicial systems become paper-thin.

McCluskey continued by drawing comparisons with the United States model, as Simon Lee and Michael Zander both do. Do we want to be like the Americans in this way? Is the argument that is frequently adduced to explain why other legal systems have Bills of Rights – because they defend the native inhabitants from the removal of their rights by new, white settlers – not applicable to Britain because we have no native non-white population? Yet we have new black and brown citizens who arguably have less than whites in the way of civil rights. Is that an effective argument? Does British law truly respect the individual? Does Parliament in all circumstances do likewise? Are the judges the right people to decide, as Michael Zander suggests? Or should we adopt Simon Lee's compromise proposal, very similar to Anthony Lester's original one in 1968, of a Constitutional Committee, similar to the French Conseil Constitutionnel, made up of 'not only the senior judges but also senior politicians and perhaps . . . the kind of people who head Royal Commissions and Committees of Inquiry' and others.

Is this a workable idea, preferable to a straight Bill of Rights enforceable in the courts? Would it fall down because of lack of clout, or because it would not give the individual citizen the right to claim that his or her fundamental rights or freedoms were being denied? The debate rests at this point, and yet it is being picked up again with urgency by some of those on the political left who see the Zircon affair, the spy-satellite film made by Duncan Campbell for the BBC, as a particularly gross example of the infringement of the rights of the individual by the state. Such observers have come to accept the idea of a Bill of Rights in the hope that it would prevent such things as the raids on the *New Statesman*'s offices, on BBC Scotland's offices in Glasgow and on the homes of the journalists involved.

Is Lord McCluskey right when he opposes such views? He says:

> To enact a Bill of Rights in noble language and to set judges to apply it to cases would, I suspect, be the modern equivalent of writing and producing a modern morality play. It would be entertaining, even instructive, and would allow us to applaud the occasional triumph of those values the scriptwriters favoured. But it would have little effect on how people behaved in the real world.*

Or is Peter Kellner right in arguing that, had there been a Bill of Rights in Britain (and he was suggesting that *New Statesman* readers and Labour MPs should back the Gardner Bill on 6 February 1987), the Zircon affair would have been handled quite differently? For he argues:

---

*Reith Lectures, 20 November 1986.

Let us imagine that Sir Edward's Bill was already on the statute book. The Special Branch arrive at the BBC's Scottish headquarters in Glasgow. They produce their warrant in conformity with the Official Secrets Act and the Police and Criminal Evidence Act. Under the Human Rights Act the BBC's lawyers would be able to test the warrant in a far more fundamental way than they were able to do last Sunday.

Article 10 of the Convention states that: Everyone has the right to freedom of expression. This right shall include freedom to hold opinions and to receive and impart information and ideas without interference by public authority and regardless of frontiers.

Last weekend's raid on the BBC violated its right both to receive and impart information. . . . By removing the transmission copies of all of Duncan Campbell's films (and not just the one on the Zircon project), it violated the BBC's right to impart information.

Suppose the BBC's lawyers had armed themselves with this article of the Convention and sought an injunction to restrain the Special Branch from proceeding with their search. The lawyers working for the security services would presumably have based their claim to continue the search on paragraph two of Article 10:

The exercise of these freedoms, since it carries with it duties and responsibilities, may be subject to such formalities, conditions, restrictions or penalties as are prescribed by law and are necessary in a democratic society, in the interests of national security, territorial integrity or public safety.*

Kellner suggests that the state would have upheld its right to raid offices at weekends 'in the interests of national security' but argues that the qualification of restrictions as 'are

---

*'Civil Liberties: Overcoming the SEJ Factor', *New Statesman*, 6 February 1987.

necessary in a democratic society' would have to be tested. So if the BBC had been able to fight the search warrant under a Human Rights Act,

> a judge would have had three options. He could have held an immediate hearing and found for the Special Branch; or held an immediate hearing and found for the BBC; or stopped the search, ordered the BBC not to move or destroy any of the material relating to Campbell's programmes, and ordered a full-scale hearing of the issue of whether the search was lawful.*

Thus it might be that the government's right to raid material gathered by 'journalists it doesn't like' would be upheld by a Human Rights Act, but at least the appropriate questions could have been asked. The state would have been challenged to provide evidence that the raid really was in the interests of national security and that the restrictions were necessary in a democratic society. This process would strengthen the hand of those who wanted to publish or to screen.

Simon Lee addresses this point in discussing the ban on trade union membership at GCHQ, the government communications headquarters at Cheltenham. As he says, the Law Lords decided to uphold Mrs Thatcher's ban (which had taken place without consultation, since she felt that 'national security would be imperilled by negotiation'). Similarly, he argues, there is little reason to believe that the police raid on BBC Glasgow in connection with the Zircon programme would have been condemned by judges interpreting a Bill of Rights: 'there is little reason to suppose that judges who defer to claims of national security as in the Law Lords decision or in the granting of the Glasgow warrant, would somehow intervene more readily under the umbrella of a Bill of Rights'. This is because national security is an exception to the rights contained in the Convention. In support of Lee's viewpoint is the fact that 'the European Commission rejected the GCHQ

---

*Ibid.

unions' claim that the ban on trade union membership at GCHQ violated their right under Article 11 of the Convention. Thus the unions' case did not even reach the European Court, since it could not pass the first stage of convincing the Commission that there was a case to answer.'

Official Secrets and Freedom of Information

There has been a remarkable amount of cross-party political agreement about the issue of national security, as well as a willingness of opposition parties to go along with the government's view of what does or does not constitute a threat to national security. Neil Kinnock gave an interview to the *New Statesman* in the wake of the Zircon affair, when the *New Statesman*'s offices had been raided by the Special Branch, and was asked: 'When the Prime Minister asked you to back her on a "grave issue of national security", did you have any choice?' Kinnock replied:

> Well, this leader of the opposition doesn't choose to make a choice in those circumstances. The information available in some cases days, in some cases weeks, after that Thursday (22 January) was not available then, and we could have been talking, of course, about the most critical issue. And on that basis, as I said in a statement that I made at nine o'clock that morning, the decision is to take their word for it until there is proof to the contrary.

Meanwhile Alan Protheroe, the Assistant Director-General of the BBC, took up the cudgels against that kind of attitude. 'L'Affaire Zircon', as he described it, had a devastating effect on the BBC. He regarded the Special Branch seizure of all material relating to the projected TV series 'Secret Society' as 'a shabby, shameful, disgraceful state-sponsored incursion into a journalistic establishment'. Is there a right to know, he asked, and why has the Official Secrets Act 1911 not yet been superseded? He continued:

> Despite my firm belief in the overwhelming need for a UK Freedom of Information Act to dissipate the paranoiac fervour for excessive secrecy that besets governments in this country (even a Civil Service internal telephone directory is a classified document), I believe, with equal vigour, that no journalist, journalistic organisation or citizen has any 'right' to disclose a state secret. And there, of course, is the problem: determining what is and what is not a 'state secret'. Even more acutely, what is a *real* 'state secret': what information, what knowledge will constructively aid an enemy bent on the destruction of this country.*

'Give me the liberty to know, to utter, and to argue freely, according to conscience, above all liberty,' said Milton in his *Areopagitica* (1644). The poet's words, nearly three hundred and fifty years on, are just beginning to be taken seriously. The 'right to know' has become an establishment concept. The campaign for a Freedom of Information Act has the support of such uncontroversial figures as Sir Douglas Wass, Sir Patrick Nairne and Alan Protheroe of the BBC. The consensus is growing that a Freedom of Information Act is required, and the commitment to reform or replace the Official Secrets Act, with its notorious catch-all Section 2, has been made by all parties while in opposition, including the Conservatives, who have used the Act in government more than any other party.

The history of the Act itself is, as Clive Ponting points out in his contribution to this book, instructive. On 1 July 1911 the German gunboat *Panther* was sent to Agadir in Morocco. Its stated purpose was to subdue a native uprising which threatened German interests there, but it was in fact attempting to protect Germany's position in North Africa after a series of undercover deals between France, Spain and Britain.

The Listener, 12 February 1987.

Britain had agreed to turn in the other direction while France and Spain carved up the territory between them, in exchange for a promise of no interference in British activities in Egypt. The Agadir incident nearly gave rise to war, and the British government of the day decided that many of the problems surrounding the business had come about because of too great a leakage of information. It decided to tighten up the security legislation with some draconian measures. The result was the passing, in August 1911, of the Official Secrets Act in thirty minutes flat: shades of the 1914 Aliens Act, and indications perhaps that the government felt less than secure and that Parliament could easily be panicked. Every time an MP stood up to make a speech in opposition to the new Act he was forcibly dragged down into his seat.

The then Under-Secretary of State for War, Colonel J. E. B. Seely, said that 'none of His Majesty's loyal subjects run the least risk whatever of having their liberties infringed in any degree or particular'. However, as Alan Protheroe wrote in his *Listener* article: 'within months, as Dr Nicholas Hiley of New Hall, Cambridge, recalls in a note to me, the War Office had begun to examine the new Act as a means of controlling the press'.*

The Official Secrets Act gained an increasingly poor reputation. It is perceived as being full of holes even by those, such as John Ranelagh in his essay in this book, who do not advocate removing it. In 1971 the Franks Committee was set up to investigate the Act's notorious Section 2. This section is the one that everybody joining the Civil Service has to sign – whether they are, as Clive Ponting puts it, 'a top mandarin in Whitehall, a gardener at Hampton Court Palace or a cleaner.' Section 2 governs every item of information in Whitehall, 'from the most mundane (the number of paperclips ordered or the menu in the canteen) to the most important (the design of nuclear weapons or the next Budget), in exactly the same way'.

---

*Ibid.

The Franks Committee recommended the replacement of Section 2 with an Official Information Bill and expressed itself concerned about the wide-ranging reference of the existing legislation. A government Green Paper of 1979 had the objective of creating greater openness in government but came to nothing, despite the fact that the government had taken on board the Franks Committee's recommendations at the beginning of the 1970s:

> We found Section 2 a mess. Its scope is enormously wide. Any law which impinges on the freedom of information in a democracy should be much more tightly drawn. A catch-all provision is saved from absurdity in operation only by the sparing exercise of the Attorney-General's discretion, and the inevitably selective way in which it is exercised gives rise to considerable unease.

Franks concluded that the criminal law should deal in future only with the disclosure of information classified as 'secret' or above.

After this discredited Act had yet again been used in connection with the Zircon affair, Alan Protheroe asked: 'An Act conceived in panic, weaned in apathy, nurtured in illogicality, flourishing in contempt, aged in gracelessness: why is it still on the statute book in 1987?'*

The reasons are manifold and deeply political. Both our contributors on this subject, Clive Ponting and John Ranelagh, stress the British obsession with secrecy. But, although both support a Freedom of Information Act, their suppositions are different and their aims divergent. John Ranelagh regards the obsession as dangerous because he feels that secrecy and ill-informed consensus have something to do with the British decline. In his view, the questions which are asked of politicians and civil servants are not whether any particular decision was the right one, but rather whether it fitted into the

---

*Ibid.

broad consensus and set no challenges. For that reason, he argues, there is a need for a Freedom of Information Act, although he is careful to exclude defence and national security issues from such an Act. Civil servants and politicians would have to give an account of how they came to their decisions on matters affecting the general public, such as financial issues, and the arena from which they drew advice would also therefore be made clear. The internal consensus within the Civil Service would be threatened by this, for the roots of the thinking would then be open to public scrutiny, and the convention by which the Civil Service denies an incoming administration access to the previous government's papers would presumably no longer apply.

Ranelagh does not favour the US system of 'checks and balances' held constitutionally between the legislature, the judiciary and the executive. He believes that the founding fathers of the American Revolution established this consciously, 'seeing in the resulting emotions a powerful and natural opposition to the United States ever developing an overweening government. In the fiercely competitive democratic arena of US politics, as a consequence, power is associated with publicity.' Had he said 'information' rather than 'publicity', this would have been one of the classic arguments for the abolition of the Official Secrets Act – that it gives the government of the day too much power to decide which perceived 'secrets' it is prepared to let the public know. Journalists and the public, for instance, have no right even to be party to the decision about which areas should be kept secret.

A civil servant, whose access to information may well be considerable, also has no right to decide which matters seriously affect national security and which are being kept back in the purely party-political interests of the government. Here is the nub of the issue. If the present system continues, as John Ranelagh thinks appropriate only in the specific arena of defence and national security, how is the decision to be made as to whether an issue really does concern national security, or whether there has not in fact been some awful bungle and a political cover-up is in operation? Cynics could argue that this is the case with the alleged massive spending on the Zircon project (well in excess of the £250 million limit set by the Public Accounts Committee). Cynics could also say that the government's handling of the Peter Wright case in Australia has shown that trusting ministers and their civil servants to evaluate the 'national interest' fairly is no longer a sustainable option. If the security services are to be protected by the Official Secrets Act, or by some future Freedom of Information Act which would protect them from unreasonable public scrutiny, should there not be some kind of special commission to oversee the maintenance of a security policy in the public interest and with public confidence? Sir Robert Armstrong's confession in the Wright case that he had been 'economical with the truth' cannot be a satisfactory basis for public confidence.

There is a parallel between the arguments used by Simon Lee on the one hand and John Ranelagh on the other, as there is between the views of Michael Zander and Clive Ponting. Lee and Ranelagh share doubts about the suitability of the United States type of constitutional thinking, with its strong emphasis on open government and freedom of the individual, for transplantation into the UK system. Both analyse the British constitution, see dangers within it and are prepared to make compromises. But neither sees the role of the courts as being at the forefront of this.

Zander and Ponting meanwhile argue hard for reform. Each has his doubts as to the efficacy of what he recommends. As Clive Ponting expresses it: 'The quality of life and government in Britain beyond a Freedom of Information Act would depend on the mechanisms for holding the government and the bureaucracy to account. Only when government is not only more open but also more accountable will the real benefits of freedom of information begin to be seen.' John Ranelagh would perhaps only partly disagree, but in that partial disagreement lies a world of difference; for he would exclude defence and national security, even though many members of the public and the press regard those areas as being of vital public interest. As the lobby system for off-the-record government briefing of journalists breaks down (the *Guardian* and *Independent* newspapers take no part in it), the government may gradually find it more difficult to be selective in the 'secret' information it wishes to impart. Who will decide what is in the public interest, and how will we know that the decision was made with the genuine public interest at heart, rather than party-political motive? The debate is not over yet, and what was previously thought to be a 'tired' issue has become increasingly lively. Zander, Lee, Ranelagh and Ponting all put clear cases. Whether there will be any change once a general election has taken place remains to be seen.